Vietnam Anti-War Movement

The Great American Con Job

Joe Abodeely

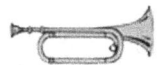

Desert Bugle Press
P.O. Box 1065
Maricopa, AZ 85139

ISBN (print) 978-0-9915286-2-2
ISBN (ebook) 978-0-9915286-3-9
LCCN: 2020919942

Special thanks to the Everett Collection, Kent State University,
Temple University, Jearld Moldenhauer, and Robert Lutz
and others for use of their photos.

See page 201 for detailed photo credits.

Vietnam Anti-War Movement — The Great American Con Job.
©2020, Joseph E. Abodeely. All rights reserved. v. 1.0

The publisher supports the value of copyright. Copyright fuels creativity, encourages diverse voices, promotes free speech, and creates a vibrant culture. Thank you for purchasing authorized editions of this book and by complying with copyright laws. Scanning, uploading, or distributing this book without permission is a theft of the author's intellectual property. If you would like permission to use material from this book (other than for review purposes) please contact the publisher.

While the information in this book is believed to be true and accurate at the date of publication, neither the author nor the editor nor the publisher can accept any legal responsibility for any errors or omissions that may be made. The publisher makes no warranty, expressed or implied, with respect to the material contained herein. The publisher is not responsible for the websites (or their content) that are not owned by the publisher.

Author exercised reasonable due diligence in determining ownership of photos used in this book. Copyrighted photos are credited. Every effort has been made to trace all copyright holders, but if any have been overlooked, the publisher will be pleased to include any necessary credits in any subsequent reprint or edition.

Vietnam Anti-War Movement — The Great American Con Job
is available at special quantity discounts when purchased in bulk.
Please email the author at JoeAbo7@gmail.com or visit him on the web at
www.JoeAbo.com for more information.

*This book is dedicated to my wife, Donna,
who has comforted, nursed, advised, cared for, and
tolerated me for fifty years.*

*It is also dedicated to those patriotic
men and women who served their country and
who are proud of their service defending South Vietnam
against Communist aggression and expansion in
Southeast Asia.*

Table of Contents

Some Truth About Vietnam 1
I Wanted to Serve 4
Geopolitical History 12
Synopsis of U.S. Involvement in Vietnam 16
Anti-War Movement and Protests 25
Who Was Against the Vietnam War and Why? 35
Academia Disinformation 85
Civil Rights Movement and Events 89
Key Vietnam War Battles 101
Firefight Near Hue 129
The End Of The Siege At Khe Sanh Combat Base 147
Air Cavalry Goes to Khe Sanh 151
Media and the War 177
Historians and the War 185
Epilogue 192
About the Author 197
Recommended Reading 199
Credits 201

Group from the University of Pennsylvania seem ready to support the President in Vietnam War and draft. Philadelphia, PA.

Some Truth About Vietnam

Why was and is the Vietnam War still so controversial? It is barely taught in schools; and what is portrayed is that America was the aggressor in the war, Ho Chi Minh was a hero, the anti-war movement was a "principled cause," and U.S. soldiers were war criminals because their involvement in the war was illegal. My replies follow.

America was not the "aggressor." Presidents Truman, Eisenhower, Kennedy, Johnson, Nixon, and Ford recognized that the region was vulnerable, and Communist expansion was a threat which violated (SEATO), the Southeast Asia Treaty Organization treaty, which included France and its protectorate—Vietnam.

Ho Chi Minh was an ardent Communist who led brutality against fellow Vietnamese people. He was a "hero" only to the Communists, their supporters, and the anti-war crowd.

The "anti-war movement" occurred at a time of

the convergence of several emerging "movements"—Civil Rights and Black Power, Women's Liberation, Gay Rights, Chicano Power, Jews and Catholics against the war. The media and academia relished the controversy as television quickly spread the carnage of the war and the debates about it to a curious public. They all took a "principled stand" against this war—and defamed anyone involved or supporting it. So-called scholars perverted and misrepresented the war's history.

While anti-war protesters acted out, U.S. Soldiers, Marines, Sailors, Airmen, and Coastguardsmen served, fought, and died in Vietnam. Women also served as nurses and administrative personnel in Vietnam; some gave their lives, too. Vietnam veterans were treated as war criminals, were mocked, called baby killers, denied jobs, and generally defamed and ostracized. Two-thirds of their age group had volunteered to serve, as opposed to one-third who volunteered during World War II. They were patriots.

Why should you care about what I think? Because you should care about the truth of the times and the service of those who served in the Vietnam War! I am one of them. I was well-educated when I served as a combat infantry officer, recorded my thoughts and actions in a diary, saw a lot of combat during the bloodiest year of the war, and later became an attorney. I am one of those Vietnam veterans speaking out for those who may have been dissuaded to defend our service.

The controversy of the Vietnam War will continue long after this presentation because how can those who maligned Vietnam veterans admit their great sin against an entire generation who served their country? They can't and they won't!

I Wanted to Serve

In 1916, Poncho Villa, a Mexican revolutionary, raided Columbus, New Mexico, killing many Americans. My grandpa was in General Pershing's Expeditionary Forces in 1916-1917 tasked to capture or kill Villa who was considered to be a bandit by some and a hero by others. Grandpa had stories of service on the Arizona-Mexico border as he lectured that a cavalryman's two best friends were his rifle and horse. He would say, "Give the water in your canteen to your horse first." Grandpa was in the 1st Cavalry, and he rode horses. Half a century later, I was in the 1st Cavalry, and I rode helicopters. Other relatives had served, so I felt obligated to serve.

I was born in 1943 in Tucson, Arizona; and as a little boy, I grew up hiking, shooting, and playing "Army" rather than "cowboys," in the desert. I had a BB gun to shoot plastic toy soldiers. My education from grade school to law school was in Tucson. I was captain of the University of Arizona wrestling team and graduated with an English B.A., and a split minor in speech and sociology. In 1965, I graduated as Army ROTC "Distinguished Military Graduate" and commissioned as 2nd Lieutenant, Infantry. I added a semester of business graduate school, a year of law school, and in 1967, I went on active duty. I knew I was going to Vietnam, was patriotic, and wanted to be a leader of men in combat. Maybe down deep inside my psyche, I just wanted to test or prove myself in man's ultimate "game"—war. Be careful what you wish for!

On Active Duty as an Infantry Lieutenant, I went to eight weeks of Combat Platoon Leaders Course training at Fort Benning, Georgia—weapons, physical fitness, patrolling, map-reading, train-fire, leadership, etc. After a weeklong break, I went to Fort Polk, Louisiana, for several months to train troops. I was scared and unsure I would return from "across the pond." I had orders to go, and this was real now. All my previous bravado had disappeared. I was 24 years old and not married; and I lived life like a condemned man during my 30-day leave of binge-drinking and "lust" before reporting for transport "across the pond." My Ma and Dad took me to the airport, and my mother could see the concern on my face and said, "Don't worry, you'll come back." I flew to Travis AFB, and then flew on to the Republic of Vietnam.

I arrived in Vietnam the first week in January 1968 (a few weeks before Tet) and was assigned as a combat infantry unit commander (platoon leader) in the 2nd battalion, 7th Cavalry, 1st Cavalry Division (Airmobile)—the first helicopter division in the Army. We were "infantry" in helicopters doing traditional "cavalry" tactics (Cavalry raids—air assaults, "search and destroy," flanking, screening, blocking, and reconnaissance), using helicopters instead of horses.

We operated around Bon Song, Hue, Khe Sanh, the A Shau Valley, and Quan Loi during my tour (January 1968-January 1969). It's a shame the Army took that

I am standing (far left) with my platoon back at Camp Evans.

mission from the 1st Air Cavalry who actually did cavalry tactics. This insulted the unit which initiated air mobility in Vietnam. Helicopters are now ubiquitous in the military.

The Tet Offensive started January 30-31, and I learned that combat was serious business and that I could get killed. I served with young men who were drafted, had no college education, came from farms or the inner city, were black, brown, poor white, "hillbilly," Puerto Rican; but they were the best soldiers the U.S. ever had. They trusted me to keep them alive, and I did.

I have never had so much responsibility for life and property as I did in Vietnam, and I never lost a man. I'm not going to feign humility; I was an excellent combat infantry unit commander.

My Company Commander said in my Officer Evaluation Report (OER) for 9 JAN to 10 MAR 68:

> *As a rifle platoon leader, Lieutenant Abodeely has conducted many platoon size operations which include night ambushes, search and clear, search and destroy and every other basic tactical technique used by a platoon. In addition to these platoon sized operations he has also participated in innumerable company operations. Some of*

these operations include cross attachment with the ARVN troops.

Lieutenant Abodeely has unerring knowledge of basic infantry tactics. In addition to his exceptional basic knowledge, Lieutenant Abodeely has illustrated uncanny ability in land navigation and map orientation. This unique bit of perception appeared to give him an unusual ability at times to diagnose the enemy's intentions before they fully materialized...

I have observed, on numerous occasions, Lieutenant Abodeely's exceptional ability to react with equanimity and force under conditions of duress. He is a fearless leader and an inspiration to those who follow him. His primary concern, secondary to the mission, is the welfare and protection of those who follow him. Case in point, I watched him move into an open area, under heavy enemy fire, to pull two wounded men to safety...

I saw action during the bloodiest year of the war in the unit that saw the most combat. Upon returning home after my one-year tour, I was astonished and

Vietnam Anti-War Movement—the Great American Con Job

1st Lieutenant Joe Abodeely in front of Battalion S-4 bunker, Camp Evans, Vietnam.

chagrined to see firsthand the public's disrespect for those risking their lives for our country.

I have practiced law for nearly 50 years (city, state, federal, and military courts), founded the Arizona Military Museum, serving as its chief executive officer for over 40 years, presented annual dinners commemorating Vietnam veterans' service, and have been an outspoken advocate for those who honorably served in the Vietnam War. I am proud to be a Vietnam veteran as are most Vietnam veterans.

My book, *Dear Mom and Dad, Love From Vietnam* earned three Global E-book Awards). This is my second book.

Maybe, my experiences playing, hiking, and shooting in the desert, and being captain of the wrestling team may have helped prepare me somewhat. After my year's tour of duty in January 1969, I returned home, finished law school, and practiced law. Since my return from Vietnam, I have tried to educate whoever would listen about the combat soldier's ordeal in the Vietnam War from a literate, firsthand perspective. The dynamics and results of the anti-war movement distorted much of the truth about the war, the reasons for it, and the service of those who fought in it.

Many who served in the war do not know or understand the complexities of it, and perhaps they justifiably do not care, but for those who may care, this perspective is for you.

What is presented here will probably not end the Vietnam War debates, but it may give some insight into that era. It is biased in favor of U.S. action and Vietnam veterans' service in the war, but this view has as much merit as one presented by a pseudo-scholar-"historian" who dodged the draft.

Geopolitical History

The history of the Vietnam War has been corrupted and misrepresented by media, journalists, historians, movies, and authors who catered to an angry discordant mood of the times rather than to facts. The war has been portrayed as a U.S. debacle, a loss, and unwarranted; the soldiers in the war have been portrayed as crazed, misfits, losers, drug addicts, or victims. Those who protested the war have been portrayed as heroes, or patriots, imbued with superior knowledge of the geopolitics of the times. Many of those misguided perceptions survive today.

After World War II—NATO and SEATO, international treaties, were created to protect regions of interest for their signatories. SEATO (Southeast Asia Treaty Organization) and the Gulf of Tonkin incident legally obligated the U.S. to act in Vietnam and prevent the expansion of Communism in the region. Five U.S. Presidents acted to protect South Vietnam, a French protectorate, and Southeast Asia from Communist

Five U.S. Presidents acted to protect South Vietnam.

aggression and expansion, because after World War II, Communist expansion was a worldwide threat. That was the mood of the United States at that time.

Vietnam was a French colony since the 1850s because the French had colonized Vietnam, neighboring Laos, and Cambodia in the mid-19th century. In the 1860s, the French government under Napoleon III first conquered southern and then central Vietnam. The central portion of the country they ruled was called the protectorate of Annam.

In August 1883, the Vietnamese court signed a treaty that turned northern Vietnam (named Tonkin by the French) and central Vietnam (named Annam, based on an early Chinese name for the region) into French protectorates. Ten years later the French annexed Laos and added it to the so-called Indochinese Union, which the French created in 1887. The region had a dual system of French and Vietnamese administration. The Nguyen Dynasty still nominally ruled Annam, with a puppet emperor residing in Hue.

Joe Abodeely

On May 19, 1941, Ho Chi Minh, an ardent Communist, organized the Viet Minh, a national independence coalition, and pushed for reunification of North and South Vietnam, ignoring that South Vietnam was an independent state. World War II started seven months later for the United States who recognized two major camps or philosophies—Communism and the so-called "free world" led by the U.S. The Communist scare was prevalent; and the Soviet Union and its satellites—China, Europe, Latin America, and elsewhere—were perceived threats. Ho Chi Minh was not a welcomed actor on the stage as far as the U.S. was concerned.

In November 1944, Harry S. Truman was elected Vice President of the United States. Truman had been vice president for less than three months when President Roosevelt died in April 1945. Despite his inexperience in foreign policy, Truman soon proved himself to be a strong-willed president. He oversaw the final months of World War II and gave orders for the detonation of two atomic bombs over Japan. Ho Chi Minh helped the U.S. against the Japanese, but Truman's government refused to recognize Ho Chi Minh's 1945 declaration of Vietnamese independence.

The United Nations came into existence in October 1945, a month after Japan surrendered in World War

II. France was an U.S. ally in World War II and a "permanent member" of the U.N. Security Council—not a minor issue in the "new world order."

In 1947, Truman promised American help for other nations resisting Communist aggression and infiltration because he despised Communism and Communist leaders, particularly Soviet dictator, Joseph Stalin.

Truman supported the restoration of a pro-French government in Indochina. This position, later called the Truman Doctrine, would underpin U.S. foreign policy during the Cold War. He was the first U.S. President to accept the Domino Theory and take steps to contain Communist expansion.

In 1948, the protectorate was merged in the Provisional Central Government of Vietnam, which was replaced the next year by the newly established State of Vietnam. Vietnam was a geopolitical pawn in the chess game between the U.S. and the Communists; hence, U.S. involvement in Vietnam stemmed from a combination of factors—Truman's interests, France's long colonial history in French Indochina, the U.S. war with Japan in the Pacific, and both Joseph Stalin's and Mao Tse-tung's pledge in 1950 to support Ho Chi Minh and the Viet Minh's guerrilla forces.

Synopsis of U.S. Involvement in Vietnam

Beginning in 1950, U.S. involvement in Southeast Asia increased from assisting French forces to providing direct military assistance to the associated states of Annam, Tonkin, Laos, and Cambodia. In May 1950, Truman committed 10 million U.S. dollars in military aid and established the Defense Attaché Office in Saigon to support anti-Communist forces in Vietnam.

In September 1950, the U.S. military advisory effort in Vietnam had a modest beginning when the United States Military Assistance Advisory Group (MAAG) Vietnam, was established in Saigon. Its mission was to supervise the issuance and employment of $10 million of military equipment to support French Legionnaires combating Viet Minh forces. In 1951-52, U.S. military assistance and advisors were sent to Vietnam, and Truman's position was that the U.S. was helping the Vietnamese stop Communism rather than helping the French keep a colony.

The robust Communist-led guerrilla insurgency, the Viet Minh, had gained widespread popular support since its inception in 1941; and this resistance continued. The French, with U.S. support, tried to reoccupy Vietnam. The U.S. military aid jumped to over $350 million by 1953 and was used to replace the badly worn World War II vintage equipment that France, economically suffering from the devastation of that war, was still using.

In 1953, Dwight Eisenhower became U.S. President, and he saw the fall of French Indochina and the threat of Communist expansion in Southeast Asia as the Domino Theory *(if South Vietnam fell, all Southeast Asia would fall).*

In 1954, France's efforts to maintain control over the South ended when the Viet Minh defeated the French at Dien Bin Phu. The 1954 Geneva Agreement ended the colonial war, granted independence to South Vietnam, and divided Vietnam at the 17th parallel pending unifying elections in 1956. Also in 1954, Diem returned at Bao Dai's request to be prime minister of a U.S.-backed government in what in the following year would be proclaimed as the Republic of Vietnam (South Vietnam).

In September 1954, right after the Geneva Accords

were signed on July 20, 1954, dividing Vietnam into north and south at the 17th parallel, President Dwight D. Eisenhower wrote to Ngo Dinh Diem, the new Prime Minister of the Bao Dai government, promising United States support to ensure a non-Communist Vietnam. The seeds of the NLF were several thousand Communists who defied the terms of the Geneva Accords (1954) and remained underground in South Vietnam.

The United States blocked the elections from taking place because the Viet Minh did not leave the south and return to the north above the 17th parallel as required by the 1954 Geneva Agreement, and South Vietnam feared a Communist victory because the Viet Minh who stayed in the south terrorized the populace, thereby preventing a fair election. Diem refused to carry out the 1954 Geneva Accords, which had called for free elections to be held throughout Vietnam in 1956 in order to establish a national government. With the south torn by dissident groups and political factions, Diem established an autocratic regime.

In January 1955, direct U.S. aid to South Vietnam began, and American advisors began arriving in February to train the South Vietnamese army. In early 1955, Diem had consolidated his control by suppressing the religious sects in the Mekong Delta and brutally suppressing unrest in Saigon. Diem defeated Bao Dai in a government-controlled referendum in October 1955, ousted the emperor, and made himself president of South Vietnam.

In December 1960, the Viet Cong was the military arm of the Communist-led National Liberation Front (NLF), an underground Communist insurgency formed to be active in South Vietnam, and they terrorized and infiltrated the Vietnamese people under Diem. In May 1961, Kennedy decided to send 500 more military advisers to Vietnam, bringing American forces there to 1,400. With an increased budget and American boots on the ground in Vietnam by 1961, segments of the U.S. government

Joint operations between US special forces and government Vietnamese forces against the Vietcong.

Vietnamese troops helicopter airlifted to attack Viet Cong.

and others among the U.S. populace began questioning these actions. In May 1963, Communists infiltrated and agitated the discontent against long-standing religious discrimination with mass Buddhist protests. Diem, an ardent Roman Catholic, did not accede to various demands from the Buddhists; and U.S. journalists did not think Diem was liberal enough in dealing with the press and Buddhist protesters.

Diem was extremely independent and did not kowtow to the Communists, Buddhists, or the United States; but to make matters worse, Diem's police allegedly killed Buddhist protesters after the police had received gunfire. The U.S. press did not believe Diem's claim that

Vietnam Anti-War Movement—the Great American Con Job

Monks and students demonstrate against the government's discriminatory, anti-Buddhist policies, Saigon, 1963.

the Communists infiltrated the Buddhists and started shooting, which the Communists later admitted that they did. This was the fuse that set off the dynamite. Buddhists were outraged, and some Buddhist generals in Diem's regime called President Kennedy to request permission to "remove" Diem.

On November 1, 1963, the Buddhist generals got JFK's approval to kill Diem and his brother in a coup three weeks before JFK's assassination. Although there is good evidence that Diem was not at fault, it did not matter. Kennedy gave the permission, and the generals assassinated Diem. The successful *coup d'état* was the culmination of nine years of autocratic and nepotistic family rule in South Vietnam under Diem, and the region became more unstable in his absence.

President Johnson expanded U.S. troop increases and decided not to run again. American public opinion did not want the U.S. involved in Vietnam, and the anti-war movement grew. Some say that Vietnam was "Nixon's war," but issues related to Vietnam started with Truman (Democrat).

After Kennedy's assassination in 1963, President Johnson began a bombing campaign against North Vietnam in August 1964 and ordered American combat units into South Vietnam in 1965, citing North Vietnamese support for the Viet Cong. This prompted the North Vietnamese Army to join the Viet Cong fighting in the south. U.S. troop levels in Vietnam peaked in 1968 at 540,000, with more than 300 Americans being killed every week.

General Abrams took over from General Westmoreland and implemented a pacification strategy rather than Westmoreland's attrition strategy. That strategy was working, and the ARVNs fought valiantly up until the time they were ordered to surrender (e.g., Xuan Loc, infra.).

Republican President Richard M. Nixon forced

Vietnam Anti-War Movement—the Great American Con Job

Above: US Army Helicopters hovering over Vietnamese troops after dropping them in the Mekong Delta provience, 1966. Below: Helicopters with troops heading to a landing zone.

U.S. Army Bell UH-1D helicopters airlift members during a search and destroy mission, South Vietnam, 1966.

the end of U.S. involvement in the Vietnam War after extensive bombing of North Vietnam. He wanted "peace with honor" and obtained the peace treaty in 1973 with the proviso that if the Communists violated the treaty, the U.S. would continue to supply South Vietnam with war material—weapons, ammunition, tanks, planes, fuel, etc.

U.S. forces left in 1973, and the Democrat Congress refused to honor the treaty as Communist forces renewed their attacks and eventually took over Saigon in 1975. The media misled the public by blaming the military for the war's outcome.

Anti-War Movement and Protests

The anti-war movement often consisted of draft evaders and others with recognized "legitimate" reasons for deferments, like being a conscientious objector, being a homosexual, working in a national security occupation, having a health condition, or being in a marital status or a sole provider for dependents. Many of them, who did not serve, became vocal against the war. Some who had "schizophrenic" views about service joined the Reserve or National Guard in CONUS (continental U.S.) and still avoided Vietnam. Many wanted to be counted as Vietnam era veterans, thinking being in service during the war was the same as being in Vietnam.

But there was no "equivalent service" to Vietnam service because those who served in Vietnam risked life, limb, and psyche, and most importantly, they were maligned for their service when they returned home from war. About one million of them are still alive.

As previously noted, the Civil Rights and Black Power movements intertwined with anti-war protests; and when viewed on television, they helped shape public opinion about the war.

The Vietnam anti-war movement was unprecedented in scope. Prior to the escalation of U.S. involvement in Vietnam, there had been a small peace movement based primarily on concerns around nuclear proliferation, particularly nuclear testing. This movement was primarily led by the Committee for Sane Nuclear Policy (SANE) created in 1957 and included the pacifist Committee for Nonviolent Action (CNVA), founded that same year, and Women's Strike for Peace (WSP).

The early opposition to the Vietnam War was largely restricted to pacifists and leftists empowered by the successful application of strategic nonviolent action in the U.S. Civil Rights Movement. Students for a Democratic Society (SDS) emerged in 1960, espousing a democratic socialist vision and opposition to militarism and became primarily focused on ending the war.

The first major protests began in 1964 and quickly gained strength as the war escalated. Starting at the University of Michigan, "teach-ins" on the Vietnam War modeled after seminars raising consciousness in sup-

Vietnam Anti-War Movement—the Great American Con Job

University of Michigan students teach-in at the Administration Building.

port of the Civil Rights Movement, brought in thousands of people. In addition to national protests, which attracted tens of thousands to Washington, D.C., there were acts of civil disobedience that became more widespread over time, including sit-ins on the steps of the Pentagon, draft induction centers, and railroad tracks transporting troops, as well as the public burning of draft cards.

As body counts escalated, civilian atrocities reports circulated, draft calls increased, and reported prospects of a U.S. victory dissipated, opposition increased. In particular, military conscription began to impact a growing number of working- and middle-class families and helped mobilize college students, who faced the prospects of being sent to Vietnam soon after graduation.

Recruiters for the military as well as companies associated with the war—such as Dow Chemical, the chief manufacturer of napalm—were increasingly met by protesters when they came to campuses. In 1967, 300,000 marched in New York City and 50,000 protesters descended on the Pentagon, with over 700 being arrested. A national organization of draft resisters was formed in 1967, calling itself the "Resistance," as many thousands were jailed, fled to sanctuary in Canada, or went underground.

Draft-age Americans being counseled by Mark Satin (far left) at the Anti-Draft Programme office in Toronto, August 1967.

Young people often fused political opposition with cultural experimentation, defying traditional American norms. Surveillance, smear campaigns, and staged support rallies were organized by government agencies to inhibit the growth of the movement; and media coverage was largely unsympathetic, yet by the end of 1967, public support for the war dropped to barely one-third of the population.

The nomination of pro-war candidates by the two major political parties despite widespread anti-war sentiments, combined with violent police actions against anti-war demonstrators at the Democratic National Convention in Chicago and elsewhere, served to further radicalize the anti-war movement. A countercultural group called the Yippies staged innovative actions and guerrilla theater. Radical priests raided offices of draft boards, destroying records; and prominent veterans of the civil rights struggle, including Martin Luther King, Jr., became increasingly outspoken against the war.

The news media began to become more skeptical in its war coverage, and mainstream churches and unions began to speak out more boldly. Blockades of thoroughfares and other forms of nonviolent direct action became commonplace. These pressures forced the Johnson administration to begin peace talks with the North Vietnamese and Viet Cong and to suspend the bombing of North Vietnam. Cohesion in the anti-war movement declined as many activists embraced far left ideologies, countercultural lifestyles, or finally abandoned their commitment to nonviolent tactics.

Still, three million people participated in demonstrations as part of the Moratorium on the War in October 1969, across the country, and half a million protested in Washington, D.C., the following month. President Nixon hoped that the gradual withdrawal of troops and a decline in draft rolls would diminish the anti-war movement. The U.S. decision to invade Cambodia in the spring of 1970, which resulted in large-scale protests, shattered those hopes.

When six college students were killed and dozens wounded in anti-war demonstrations at Kent State University and Jackson State University, tensions between the anti-war movement and the U.S. government escalated further. Hundreds of colleges and universities shut down from student strikes, occupations of campus buildings, and other disruptions forced a withdrawal of U.S. ground forces from Cambodia less than eight weeks after the initial invasion.

Vietnam Anti-War Movement—the Great American Con Job

Troops leaving UH-1 helicopter, September, 1971.

Desertions and mutinies within the armed forces made prosecution of the war increasingly difficult. Three-quarters of a million people marched on Washington in April 1971, followed in early May by tens of thousands of protesters attempting to shut down government operations in the nation's capital by blockading bridges and thoroughfares. Further revelations of massacres of Vietnamese civilians by U.S. troops, systematic deceptions of the public and Congress by the administration, torture of political prisoners in South Vietnam, and domestic spying on U.S. citizens, alienated the U.S. public further from U.S. government policy. Increasingly violent protests ended up alienating most Americans from the anti-war cause.

Despite a brief upsurge in protests and resumption of the air war against North Vietnam in the spring of 1972, the movement's devolution into factions and the withdrawal of most U.S. forces led to a decline in protests, but the anti-war movement pushed the United States to sign a peace treaty, withdraw its remaining forces, and end the draft in early 1973.

Continued U.S. support for the Thieu dictatorship in Saigon and the breakdown of the cease-fire led to small ongoing protests, leading Congress to finally refuse additional U.S. aid to the South Vietnamese regime. By this action, Congress violated the terms of the SEATO Treaty; and South Vietnam literally ran out of ammunition promised by the Paris Peace Accords. The NVA attacked towns and cities throughout South Vietnam until their Soviet-made tanks reached the Saigon President's palace in 1975, and the Communists took over, ending the war.

By the end of the war, the U.S. anti-war movement had amassed an impressive record of nonviolent action. After a decade of organizing, their actions included mass protests, vigils, sit-ins, occupations, and blockades, conscientious objection, draft resistance, desertion; guerrilla theater; obstruction of military recruiters, arms shipments, and personnel, petitioning and letter-writing campaigns, and destruction of draft files. The mass media was instrumental in aiding the anti-war movement. More specific Communist actions and propaganda could not have done a better job.

Who Was Against the Vietnam War and Why?

While young men were serving their country, fighting and dying in the jungles of South Vietnam, anti-war protests occurred in the United States and elsewhere. The anti-war protests were a "sign of the times," but they demoralized those who were fighting and dying in Vietnam. They say a picture is worth a thousand words. Vietnamese monks immolated themselves in protest to the Diem regime. Jane Fonda and John Kerry spoke against the war; Communist-front groups publicly protested in the U.S.; Jewish lawyers; activists; gays; labor; women; draft-age males; civil rights groups supported the anti-war movement. *Meanwhile, young men and women served in Vietnam.*

1955[1]–The very first protests against U.S. involvement in Vietnam were in 1955, when United States Merchant Marine sailors condemned the U.S. government for the use of U.S. merchant ships to transport European troops to "subjugate the native population" of Vietnam.

1963–

- May. Anti-Vietnam War protests in England and Australia

- June 11. (Born Lâm Văn Túc) was a Vietnamese Mahayana Buddhist monk who burned himself to death at a busy Saigon road intersection. Quảng Đức was protesting the persecution of Buddhists by the South Vietnamese Christian government led by Ngô Đình Diệm.

- September 21. War Resisters League starts first U.S. protest against Vietnam. War and "anti-Buddhist terrorism" by the U.S.-supported South Vietnamese regime with a demonstration at the U.S. Mission to the UN in New York City.

- October 9. WRL and other groups turn out 300 pickets against a speech by Madame Ngo Dinh Nhu at the Waldorf-Astoria in New York City.

---
1. Wikipedia list. See credits for reference.

Vietnam Anti-War Movement—the Great American Con Job

Buddhist monk protesting the government's religious policies commits ritual suicide in Siagon.

1964–

- March. A conference at Yale plans demonstrations on May 4.

- April 25. The *Internal Protector* published a pledge of draft resistance by some of the organizers.

- May 2. Hundreds of students demonstrated on New York's Times Square and from there went to the United Nations. Seven hundred marched in San Francisco. Smaller demonstrations took place in Boston, Madison, Wisconsin, and Seattle. These protests were organized by the Progressive Labor Party with help from the Young Socialist Alliance. The *May 2nd Movement* was the PLP's youth affiliate.

- May 12. Twelve young men in New York publicly burned their draft cards to protest the war—the first such act of war resistance.

- Fall. Free Speech Movement at the University of California at Berkley defended the right of students to carry out political organizing on campus. The founder: Mario Savio.

- Early August. White and black activists gathered

near Philadelphia, Mississippi, for the memorial service of three civil rights workers. Speakers bitterly spoke out against Johnson's use of force in Vietnam, comparing it to violence used against blacks in Mississippi.

- December 19. First coordinated nationwide protests against the Vietnam War included demonstrations in New York City sponsored by War Resisters League, Fellowship of Reconciliation, Committee for Nonviolent Action, the Socialist Party of America, and the Student Peace Union, and attended by 1500 people; San Francisco had 1000 people; Minneapolis, Miami, Austin, Sacramento, Philadelphia, Chicago, Washington, Boston, Cleveland, and other cities also had demonstrations..

1965–

- February 2–March. Protests at the University of Kansas, organized by the RA Student Peace Union.

- February 12–16. Anti-U.S. demonstrations in various cities in the world, "including a break-in at the U.S. embassy in Budapest, Hungary, by some 200 Asian and African students."

- March 15. A debate organized by the Inter-University Committee for a Public Hearing on Vietnam was held in Washington, D.C. Radio and television coverage.

- March 16. An 82-year-old Detroit woman named Alice Herz self-immolated to make a statement against the horrors of the war. She died ten days later.

- March 24. First SDS organized teach-in, at the University of Michigan at Ann Arbor. Three thousand students attended; the idea spread quickly.

- March. Berkeley, California: Jerry Rubin and Stephen Smale's Vietnam Day Committee (VDC) organized a huge protest of 35,000.

- April. Oklahoma college students sent out hundreds of thousands of pamphlets with pictures on them of dead babies in a combat zone to portray a message about battles taking place in Vietnam.

- April 17. The SDS-organized *March Against the Vietnam War* on Washington, D.C., was the largest anti-war demonstration in the U.S. to date with 15-20,000 people attending. Paul Potter demanded a radical change of society.

Vietnam Anti-War Movement—the Great American Con Job

- May 5. Several hundred people carrying a black coffin marched to the Berkeley, California, draft board, and 40 men burned their draft cards.

- May 21–23. Vietnam Day Committee organized large teach-in at UC Berkeley. Ten to thirty thousand attended.

- May 22. The Berkeley draft board was visited again, with 19 men burning their cards. President Lyndon B. Johnson was hanged in effigy.

- Summer. Young blacks in McComb, Mississippi, learned one of their classmates was killed in Vietnam and distributed a leaflet saying, "No Mississippi Negroes should be fighting in Viet Nam for the White man's freedom."

- June. Richard Steinke, a West Point graduate in Vietnam, refused to board an aircraft taking him to a remote Vietnamese village, stating the war "is not worth a single American life."

- June 27. *End Your Silence*, an open letter in the *New York Times* by the group *Artists and Writers Protest Against the War in Vietnam*.

- July. The Vietnam Day Committee organized mil-

Vietnam Anti-War Movement—the Great American Con Job

Rally at Selective Service to burn draft cards.

itant protest in Oakland, California, ended in an inglorious debacle when the organizers ended the march from Oakland to Berkeley to avoid a confrontation with police.

- July. A *Women Strike for Peace* delegation led by Cora Weiss met its North Vietnamese and Vietcong counterparts in Jakarta, Indonesia.

- July 30. A man from the Catholic Worker Movement was photographed burning his draft card on Whitehall Street in Manhattan in front of the Armed Forces Induction Center. His photograph appeared in *Life* magazine in August.

- October 15. David J. Miller burned his draft card at a rally held near the Armed Forces Induction Center on Whitehall Street in Manhattan. The 24-year-old pacifist, member of the Catholic Worker Movement, became the first man arrested and convicted under the 1965 amendment to the 1948 Selective Service Act.

- October 15–16. Europe, October 15–16. First *International Days of Protest*. Anti-U.S. demonstrations in London, Rome, Brussels, Copenhagen, and Stockholm.

- October 20. Stephen Lynn Smith, a student at

the University of Iowa, spoke to a rally at the Memorial Union in Iowa City, Iowa, and burned his draft card. He was arrested, found guilty, and put on three years of probation.

- October 30. Pro-Vietnam War march in New York City with 25,000.

- November 2. As thousands of employees were streaming out of the Pentagon building in Washington in the late afternoon, Norman Morrison, a thirty-two-year-old pacifist, father of three, stood below the third-floor windows of Secretary of Defense Robert McNamara, doused himself with kerosene, and set himself afire, giving up his life in protest against the war.

- November 6. Thomas C. Cornell, Marc Paul Edelman, Roy Lisker, David McReynolds, and James Wilson burned their draft cards at a public rally organized by the Committee for Non-Violent Action in Union Square, New York City.

- November 27. There was a SANE-sponsored *March on Washington* in 1965. There were 15-20,000 demonstrators.

- December 16–17. High school students in Des Moines, Iowa, were suspended for wearing black armbands to "mourn the deaths on both sides" and in support of Robert Kennedy's call for a Christmas truce. The students sued the Des Moines School District, resulting in the 1969 U.S. Supreme Court decision in favor of the students, *Tinker v. Des Moines*.

1966–From September 1965 to January 1970, 170,000 men were drafted and another 180,000 enlisted. By January, 2,000,000 men had secured college deferments.

- February. Local artists in Hollywood build a 60-foot tower of protest on Sunset Boulevard.

- March 25–26. Second *Days of International Protest*. Organized by the National Coordinating Committee to End the War in Vietnam, led by SANE, Women Strike for Peace, the Committee for Nonviolent Action and the SDS: 20,000 to 25,000 in New York alone, demonstrations also in Boston, Philadelphia, Washington, Chicago, Detroit, San Francisco, Oklahoma City. Abroad in Ottawa, London, Oslo, Stockholm, Lyon, and Tokyo.

- March 31. David Paul O'Brien and three companions burned their draft cards on the steps of the

Vietnam Anti-War Movement—the Great American Con Job

South Boston Courthouse. The case was tried by the Supreme Court as *United States v. O'Brien*.

- Spring. Clergy and Laymen Concerned About Vietnam was founded.

- May 15. *March Against the Vietnam War*, led by SANE and Women Strike for Peace, with 8-10,000 taking part.

- Muhammad Ali (Cassius Clay) refused to go to war, famously stating that he had "no quarrel with the Viet Cong" and that "no Viet Cong ever called me nigger." Ali also stated he would not go "10,000 miles to help murder, kill, and burn other people to simply help continue the domination of white slave-masters over dark people." In 1967, he was sentenced to 5 years in prison but was released on appeal by the United States Supreme Court.

- Summer. Six members of the SNCC invade an induction center in Atlanta and were later arrested.

- July. First national anti-war *Mobilization Committee* was established.

- July 3. A crowd of over 4,000 demonstrated

Vietnam Anti-War Movement—the Great American Con Job

Muhammad Ali (Cassius Clay)

Harlem Peace March to End Racial Oppression, April 27, 1967.

outside of the U.S. Embassy in London. Scuffles broke out between the protesters and police, and at least 31 people were arrested.

- November 7. Protests against Robert McNamara at Harvard University.

- Late December. Student Mobilization Committee was formed.

1967–

- January 29–February 5. *Angry Arts Week*, by the Artists Protest group.

- March 25. Vietnam March. Dr. Benjamin Spock, Martin Luther King, Jr. led nearly 5,000 marchers through the Chicago Loop to protest U.S. policy in Vietnam. March 25, 1967.

- April 4. Martin Luther King, Jr., spoke at Riverside Church in New York about the war: "Beyond Vietnam: A Time to Break Silence." King stated that *"somehow this madness must cease. We must stop now. I speak as a child of God and brother to the suffering poor of Vietnam. I speak for those whose land is being laid waste, whose homes are being destroyed, whose culture is being subverted. I speak for the poor of America who are paying the*

Vietnam Anti-War Movement—the Great American Con Job

Left: Dr. Martin Luther King. Below, King with Dr. Benjamin Spock during Vietnam protest in Chicago, March 25, 1967.

double price of smashed hopes at home and death and corruption in Vietnam. I speak as a citizen of the world, for the world as it stands aghast at the path we have taken. I speak as an American to the leaders of my own nation. The great initiative in this war is ours. The initiative to stop it must be ours."

- April 15. At Sheep Meadow, Central Park, New York City, about 60 young men including a few students from Cornell University came together to burn their draft cards in a Maxwell House coffee can. More joined them, including uniformed Green Beret Army Reservist, Gary Rader. As many as 158 cards were burned.

- April 15. *Spring Mobe* protested in New York City (300,000) and in San Francisco. Founded in November 1966 as the Spring Mobilization Committee to End the War in Vietnam. Its National director was Reverend James L. Bevel.

- May 20–21. Seven hundred activists at Spring Mobilization Conference, Washington, D.C. A National Mobilization Committee to End the War in Vietnam (the Mobe) was created.

- May and November. Sweden. *International War Crimes Tribunal.*

Vietnam Anti-War Movement—the Great American Con Job

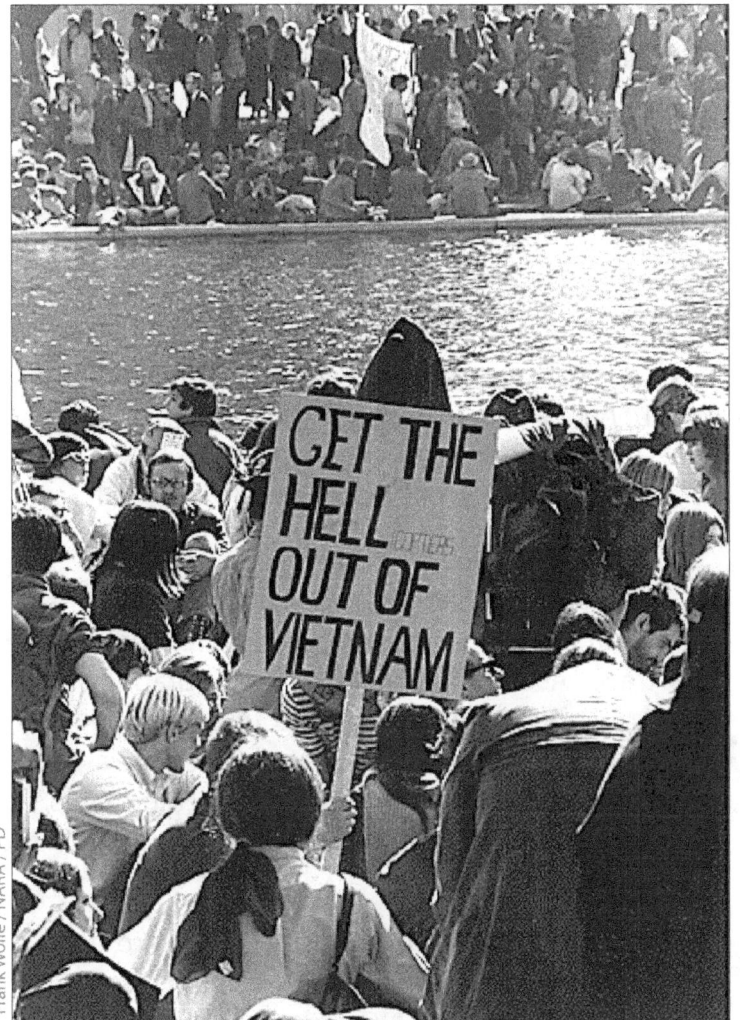

The March on the Pentagon, October 21, 1967

- June 1. The Vietnam Veterans Against the War formed. Veteran Jan Barry Crumb participated in a protest on April 7 called the *Fifth Avenue Peace Parade* in New York City. On May 30, Crumb and ten like-minded men attended a peace demonstration in Washington, D.C.

- June 23. *The Bond*, the first G.I. underground paper was established.

- June 23. Thirteen hundred police attacked 10,000 peace marchers at the Century Plaza Hotel in Los Angeles where President Lyndon B. Johnson was being honored.

- Summer of 1967. Neil Armstrong and various other NASA officials began a tour of South America to raise awareness for space travel. According to *First Man*, a biography of Armstrong's life, during the tour, several South American college students protested the astronaut, and shouted such phrases as "Murderers, get out of Vietnam!" and other anti-Vietnam War messages.

- October 16. A day of widespread war protest organized by The Mobe in 30 cities across the U.S. About 1,400 draft cards were burned.

Vietnam Anti-War Movement—the Great American Con Job

Above: Philadelphia march against the war.
Below: Resist the Draft protest march.

- October 18. *Dow Day*, University of Wisconsin–Madison. This was the first university Vietnam War protest to turn violent. Thousands of students protested Dow Chemical (maker of napalm) recruiting on campus. Nineteen police officers and about 50 students were treated for injuries at hospitals.

- October 20. Resist leaders presented draft cards to the Department of Justice, Washington, D.C.

- October 21–23. National Mobe organized *The March on the Pentagon to Confront the War Makers*. One hundred thousand congregated at the Lincoln Memorial on the D.C. Mall; 35,000 (possibly up to 50,000) went on to the Pentagon, some to engage in acts of civil disobedience. Norman Mailer's *The Armies of the Night* described the event.

- October 27. Father Philip Berrigan, a Josephite priest and World War II veteran, led a group now known as the Baltimore Four who went to a draft board in Baltimore, Maryland, drenched the draft records with blood, and waited to be arrested.

- December 4. National draft card turn in. At San

Vietnam Anti-War Movement—the Great American Con Job

National (MOBE) Mobilization to End the War in Vietnam demonstration, Washington, D.C., October 21, 1967.

Francisco's Federal Building, some 500 protesters witnessed 88 draft cards collected and burned.

- December 4–8. *Stop the Draft Week* demonstrations in New York. Five hundred and eighty-five arrested, amongst them Benjamin Spock.

- Sweden, December 20. Seventh Year of the Vietcong (the *Front National de Libération du Vietnam du Sud*, or *FNL*) celebrated with violent clashes in Stockholm. Demonstrations in 40 Swedish towns.

1968–

- German students protested against the Vietnam War in 1968.

- Peace Corps volunteers in Chile spoke out against the war. Ninety-two volunteers defied the Peace Corps director and issued a circular denouncing the war.

- January. Singer Eartha Kitt, while at a luncheon at the White House, spoke out against the war and its effects on the youth, exclaiming, "you send the best of this country off to be shot and maimed," to her fellow guests. "They rebel in the street. They will take pot...and they will get high.

Vietnam Anti-War Movement—the Great American Con Job

Anti-Vietnam War protest and demonstration in front of the White House in support of singer Eartha Kitt.

They don't want to go to school because they're going to be snatched off from their mothers to be shot in Vietnam."

- January 15. Jeannette Rankin led a demonstration of thousands of women in Washington, D.C.

- March 17. London, Sunday. There was a violent protest in London (street occupation), not supported by the Old Left. Over 300 arrests.

- April 2. Frankfurt, Germany, Gudrun Ensslin and Andreas Baader, joined by Thorwald Proll and Horst Sohnlein, set fire to two department stores.

- April 3. National draft card turn in. About 1,000 draft cards were turned in. In Boston, 15,000 protesters watched 235 men turn in their draft cards.

- April 4. Reverend Martin Luther King, Jr., assassinated.

- Late April. Student Mobe sponsored national student strike, demonstrations in New York and San Francisco.

- April–May. Occupation of five buildings at Columbia University. Future leading Weather

Vietnam Anti-War Movement—the Great American Con Job

Anti-war march toward Washington Square, Philadelphia, PA, 1968.

Dr. Martin Luther King, Jr.

Underground member Mark Rudd gained prominence.

- April 11. Berlin, Germany. Rudi Dutschke was shot and wounded. Massive riots against Axel Springer publishers.
- May. FBI's COINTELPRO campaign was launched against the New Left.
- May. Agricultural Building at Southern Illinois University (SIU) was bombed.
- May 1. Boston University graduate Philip Supina wrote to his draft board in Tucson, Arizona, that he had "absolutely no intention to report for [his] exam, or for induction, or to aid in any way the American war effort against the people of Vietnam."
- May 17. Philip Berrigan and his brother, Daniel, led seven others into a draft board office in Catonsville, Maryland, removed records, and set them afire with homemade napalm outside in front of reporters and onlookers.
- June 4–5. Robert F. Kennedy, presidential candidate, who was the hope of the anti-war

movement, was shot after winning the California primary. He died the next morning, June 6.

- Late June. Student Mobe ruptures.

- August 28. Democratic National Convention in Chicago. Violent clashes occurred.

- October 14, 1968. Presidio mutiny sit-down protest was carried out by 27 prisoners at the Presidio stockade in San Francisco, California.

- October 21. In Japan, a group of 290,000 activists occupied the Shinjuku Station, protesting an earlier incident in August 1967 where a JNR freight train hauling kerosene to the Tachikawa Airbase collided with another train and exploded. The event, known as the Shinjuku Station riots managed to disrupt all railway traffic at the station and led to clashes with riot police and acts of vandalism; it was the largest anti-war protest in Japan at the time.

- November 14. National draft card turn in.

1969–

- Major campus protests took place across the country during the whole year.

- January 19–20. Protests against Richard Nixon's inauguration.

- February 28. A group of Seattle Panthers led by Lt. Elmer Dixon gathered on the steps of the Capitol in Olympia to protest a bill that would make it a crime to exhibit firearms "in a manner manifesting an intent to intimidate others." In contrast to a California demonstration, they did not enter the building and they were not arrested.

- March 22. Nine protesters smashed glass, hurled files out a fourth floor window, and poured blood on files and furniture at the Dow Chemical offices in Washington, D.C.

- March 29. Conspiracy charges against eight suspected organizers of the Chicago Convention Protests.

- April 5–6. Anti-war demonstrations and parades in several cities, New York, San Francisco, Los Angeles, Washington, D.C. and others.

- May 21. Silver Spring Three–Les Bayless, John Bayless, and Michael Bransome walked into a Silver Spring, Maryland, Selective Service office

Vietnam Anti-War Movement—the Great American Con Job

Above: Seattle Panthers led by Lt. Elmer Dixon on the steps of the Washington State Capitol in Olympia. Below: Protesters play patriotic songs on kazoos at the anti-Vietnam War rally in DC.

where they destroyed several hundred draft records to protest the war.

- June. At Brown University commencement, two-thirds of the graduating class turned their backs when Henry Kissinger stood up to address them.

- June 8. The Old Main building at SIU burns to the ground. Units of firefighters from all over the area tried to salvage the building but could not put out the fire before everything was destroyed.

- June. Chicago. SDS national convention. The SDS disintegrates into SDS-WSA and SDS. The Worker Student Alliance of the Progressive Labor Party (PLP) has the majority of delegates (900) on its side. The smaller Revolutionary Youth Movement faction (500) divides into RYM-I/Weatherman, who retained control of the SDS National Office, and Maoist RYM-II. This faction will further divide into the various groups of New Communist Movement. There were several anti-war organizations.

- July 4–5. Cleveland. The national anti-war conference established the National Mobilization Committee to End the War in Vietnam.

Vietnam Anti-War Movement—the Great American Con Job

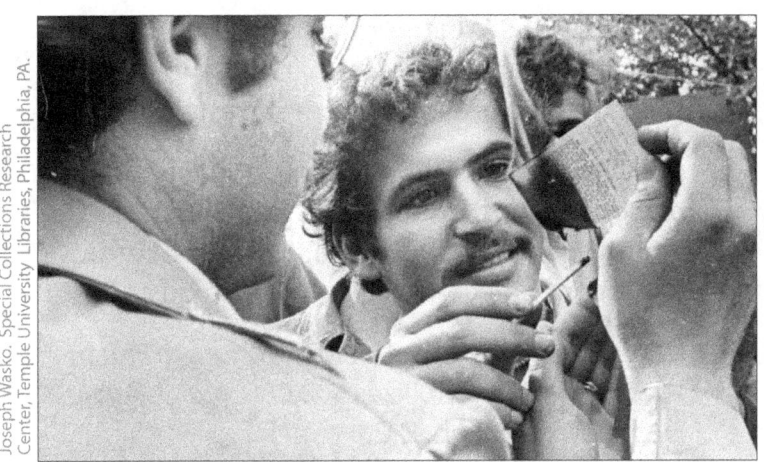

Above: Draft card burning at the Moratorium Rally at J.F.K. Plaza, 1969. Below: Crowd of Vietnam War protestors at City Hall, Philadelphia, PA, 1969.

- October 8–11. Weatherman's disastrous *Days of Rage* in Chicago. Only 300 militants show up, not the expected 10,000. 287 were arrested.

- October 15. *National Moratorium Against the War demonstrations*. Huge crowds in Washington and in Boston (100,000). Anti-war Senator, George McGovern, spoke to a large crowd in Boston.

- November 15. The *Mobe's Moratorium to End the War in Vietnam* mobilizes 500,000. *March Against Death*, Washington, D.C.

- November 15. San Francisco march.

- November 26. Draft-lottery bill signed.

- December 1. The U.S. Selective Service System conducted two lotteries.

Vietnam Anti-War Movement—the Great American Con Job

Above: Moratorium to End the War. Demonstrations against the Vietnam War took place across the United States on October 15, 1969. Below: Peace Moratorium office, 1969.

- December 7. The 5th Dimension performs their song *Declaration* on the *Ed Sullivan Show*. The opening of the Declaration of Independence (for their future security) said that it was a right and duty to revolt against despotism.

1970–

- February, March. Wave of bombings across the USA.

- March. Anti-draft protests across the USA.

- March 14. Two American merchant marine sailors named Clyde McKay and Alvin Glatkowski seized the *SS Columbia Eagle* and forced the master to sail to Cambodia as opposed to Thailand, where it was on its way to deliver napalm bombs for the U.S. Air Force in Vietnam.

- April. New Mobe Moratorium and SMC protests across the country.

- April 4. A right-wing *Victory March*, organized by Reverend Carl McIntire calls for victory in the Vietnam War. 50,000 attend.

- April 19. Moratorium announces disbanding.

- May 2. Violent anti-war rallies at many universities.

Vietnam Anti-War Movement—the Great American Con Job

Above: Viet Cong flags frame anti-Vietnam War protesters in Boston, April, 1970. Below: Members of the Chicago Conspiracy, Abbie Hoffman, Jerry Rubin (center), New Haven, CT, 1970.

- May 4. Kent State University, Ohio. Kent State Shootings—U.S. National Guard killed four young people during a demonstration. As a result, four million students went on strike at more than 450 universities and colleges. The best-known cultural response to the deaths at Kent State was the protest song *Ohio*, written by Neil Young for Crosby, Stills, Nash & Young.

- May 8. New York. *Hard Hat Riot*: after a student anti-war demonstration, workers attacked them and rioted for two hours.

- May 9. Mobe sponsored *Kent State/Cambodia Incursion Protest*, Washington, D.C. Seventy-five to 100,000 demonstrators converged on Washington, D.C., to protest the Kent State shootings and the Nixon administration's incursion into Cambodia. Even though the demonstration was quickly put together, protesters were still able to bring out thousands to march in the Capital. It was an almost spontaneous response to the events of the previous week. Police ringed the White House with buses to block the demonstrators from getting too close to the executive mansion. Early in the morning

Vietnam Anti-War Movement—the Great American Con Job

National Guard at Kent State University, May 4, 1970.

before the march, Nixon met with protesters briefly at the Lincoln Memorial.

- May 14. Jackson State College. Jackson State killings: Two dead and twelve injured during violent protests.

- May 20. New York. An estimated 60,000 to 150,000 went at a pro-war demonstration on Wall Street.

- May 28. University of Tennessee, Knoxville, TN. Nixon at Billy Graham Crusade in Neyland Stadium where 800 Students carried "Thou Shalt Not Kill" signs into the stadium. Many are arrested and charged with "disrupting a religious service" with only Republican candidates on the stage with Graham and Nixon.

- June. At commencement for the University of Massachusetts, students stenciled red fists of protests, white peace symbols, and blue doves onto their black gowns.

- August 24. University of Wisconsin–Madison. Sterling Hall bombing: aimed at the Army Math Research Center on the second, third, and fourth floors of the building. In missing its target, a Ford van packed with explosives hit the physics

Vietnam Anti-War Movement—the Great American Con Job

Above: John F. Kennedy Plaza, Philadelphia, PA, 1970. Below: Anti-Vietnam War peace march, San Francisco, California, 1970.

laboratory on the first floor and killed young researcher, Robert Fassnacht, and seriously injured another person.

- August 29. *Chicano Moratorium*. Twenty to thirty thousand Mexican-Americans participated in the largest anti-war demonstration in Los Angeles. Police are attacked with clubs and guns and kill three people, including Rubén Salazar, a TV news director and *LA Times* reporter.

1971–

- March 1. Weatherman planted a bomb in the Capitol building in Washington, D.C., causing $300,000 in damage, but no casualties.

- April. The Vancouver Indo-Chinese Women's Conference (VICWC), a six-day protest, gathered close to a thousand women.

- April 19–23. Vietnam Veterans Against the War (VVAW) staged operation *Dewey Canyon III*. A thousand camped on the National Mall.

- April 22–28. VVAW (and John Kerry) testified before Congress.

- April 24. *Peaceful Vietnam War Out Now* rally in Washington, D.C., on National Mall with 200,000

Vietnam Anti-War Movement—the Great American Con Job

John Kerry, VVAW spokesman at the microphone, 1971.

calling for an end to the Vietnam War. On the West Coast, in San Francisco, 156,000 participate in the largest demonstration so far.

- April 26. More militant attempts in Washington, D. C., to shut down the government were futile against 5,000 police and 12,000 troops.

- April 30. Anti-war protesters at the Justice Department.

- May. The Vietnam War was the longest military engagement Australia had ever participated in and many ordinary Australians were opposed to it. The demonstration in Melbourne, led by Member for Parliament Jim Cairns, saw over 100,000 people take to the streets for a peaceful occupation of the city. Across Australia, it was estimated that 200,000 people took part.

- May 3–5. *May Day Protests*. Planned by Rennie Davis and Jerry Coffin of the War Resisters League, later joined by Michael Lerner; militant mass action tried to shut down the government in Washington, D.C. Twelve thousand six hundred fourteen were arrested, a record in American history.

- August. A group of nuns, priests, and laypeople

Vietnam Anti-War Movement—the Great American Con Job

*Above: Vietnam Veterans Against the War, October 25, 1971.
Below: Melbourne, Australia. Over 200,000 people gathered across the country to protest the Vietnam War, May, 1971.*

raided a draft board in Camden, New Jersey. They came to be known as the Camden 28.

- November 6. Toronto, Canada.

1972–

- April 15–20. May. New waves of protests across the country. Eight hundred National Guardsmen were ordered onto campus.

- May 11. Frankfurt am Main, Germany, Headquarters of the V Corps at the IG Farben Building. The *Commando Petra Schelm* of the *Rote Armee Fraktion* killed U.S. Officer Paul Bloomquist and wounded thirteen in a bombing attack.

- May 21. *Emergency March* on Washington, D.C., organized by the National Peace Action Coalition and the People's Coalition for Peace and Justice. Eight to fifteen thousand protested in Washington, D.C., against increased bombing of North Vietnam and the mining of its harbors.

- May 24. Heidelberg, Germany. The Red Army Faction detonated two car bombs at the European Headquarters of the US Army, killing three.

Vietnam Anti-War Movement—the Great American Con Job

Above: Toronto protest against the war. Below: Women demonstrate for equality and against the Vietnam War. 1972.

- June 22. *Ring Around Congress* demonstration, Washington, D.C.

- In July. Jane Fonda visited North Vietnam and spoke on Hanoi Radio, earning herself the nickname "Hanoi Jane."

- August 22. Three thousand protested against the 1972 Republican National Convention in Miami Beach. Ron Kovic, a wheelchair-bound Vietnam veteran, led fellow veterans into the Convention Hall, wheeled down the aisles, and as Nixon began his acceptance speech shouted, "Stop the bombing! Stop the war!"

- October 14. The *Peace March to End the Vietnam War* was held in San Francisco. This demonstration began at City Hall and moved down Fulton Street to Golden Gate Park, where speeches were given. Over 2,000 were in attendance. Numerous groups (including veterans) marched to support the so-called "7-Point" plan to peace. George McGovern had given a speech at the Cow Palace the night before, which energized the Saturday morning event.

- November 7. General Election day. President Nixon beat George McGovern in a landslide elec-

Vietnam Anti-War Movement—the Great American Con Job

US actress and peace activist, Jane Fonda, in Hanoi. Fonda's trip to North Vietnam was part of her protest campaign against the US involvement in the Vietnam War.

tion victory, with 60.7% popular votes and 520 electoral votes.

- December. There were protests against Hanoi and Haiphong bombings.

1973–

- January 20. Second inauguration of Richard Nixon. Inauguration protests, *March Against Racism & the War* in Washington, D.C.

Academia Disinformation

Most anti-war protesters were college students from middle- or upper-class families who did not distinguish between the war and its combatants. Military Deferments or postponements to avoid Vietnam service favored the wealthy and well-educated who regarded U.S. soldiers as ready and willing killers or ignorant dupes. After all, what young man preferred to go to war than be in college?

Students who had to work their way through college on a part-time basis could not get deferments; therefore, most Vietnam veterans in the 1960s and early 1970s came from poor or working-class backgrounds. They had only high school educations; but they were the most educated veterans in U.S. history, and more than half returned to school after their war service.

Academic curricula during the 1960s and 1970s skewed the image of the war through anti-war history faculty called orthodox historians. Since Vietnam veterans or war supporters were not getting jobs in academia or journalism, this caused and influenced biased presentations of the war in schools and in the media. Even the major veterans organizations and prospective employers initially shunned Vietnam veterans, as did academia. Academia claimed diversity and thought "reasonable" people shared their anti-war view while historians who justified U.S. involvement in Vietnam were called revisionist "propagandists."

Writers like David Halberstam, Neil Sheehan, Stanley Karnow, and other "orthodox" authors wrote about the era from Vietnam's division in 1954 to Tet in 1968, and gave minimal coverage of the years 1969 to 1975.

They were actually journalists, not historians, who claimed that U.S. military fighting and the war were unlawful, unsuccessful, and not strategically important. They opined that the war caused long-term psychological damage in huge numbers of U.S. Veterans, and depicted the Republic of Vietnam's President Diem as a reactionary whose tyranny deprived his government of legitimacy.

They made the war appear reprehensible and draft dodging sensible. Their view represented the "facts" and was called "orthodox" history. But scholarship evolved as scholars in the late 1990s presented histories arguing that South Vietnam grew much stronger during 1969 to 1975.

Revisionists presented so-called revisionist history and argued that by the early 1970s South Vietnam forces had improved greatly, and with the help of the United States wiped out the VC. ARVN forces defeated a massive offensive by fourteen North Vietnamese divisions in the spring of 1972. The more recent revisionist histories were backed by extensive, well-documented research, but some college faculties refused to give due consideration to the revisionists' viewpoint. The media and anti-war crowd ignored this fact, but as documentation became more available, revisionist scholarship improved, and more truth about the war emerged.

Museums and academia continue to omit meaningful Vietnam War history and exhibits, but the "revisionist" view is still advancing as U.S. armed forces official reading lists are peppered with books by revisionists, and some of American media are providing a forum for their works.

There is still tension between Vietnam veterans and the anti-war crowd for several reasons: Vietnam veterans who saw combat lacked political influence against the powerful, educated anti-war crowd, and they blamed the negative reception they got coming home on the protesters who never served. They consider the anti-war crowd as draft dodgers and cowards, and think the anti-war types would lose face if they admitted they were egregiously wrong in defaming Vietnam veterans.

American Legion and Veterans of Foreign War members parade to Independence Hall in support of United States policy on Vietnam. Philadelphia, PA. October 24, 1965.

Civil Rights Movement and Events

One can never understand the Vietnam War without understanding U.S. domestic politics as well as the geopolitics of the times. While the U.S. supported efforts against Communist forces in Indo-China since the early 1950s, a domestic "war" brewed at home. The U.S. Civil Rights Movement was coming of age and had profound influence on the public and on other "causes" and protests against the government and the war. The Vietnam War happened at a time when there was much turmoil in the United States. As the war escalated, the Civil Rights Movement escalated as Martin Luther King, Jr., cited the war as part of the oppression of "Negroes."

Other causes like the women's liberation movement, Mexican farm workers' movement, labor movement, Jews against the war movement, Communists, and draft age men avoiding military service were factors contributing to the chaos, but the Civil Rights and Black Power Movements, intertwined in anti-war pro-

Joe Abodeely

Above: Women's liberation march from Farrugut Square to Layfette, Washington, D.C., August 26, 1970. Below: Seattle Chicanos lead Peace March, October 31, 1970.

Vietnam Anti-War Movement—the Great American Con Job

Left: Black Panther Convention, Lincoln Memorial, June 19, 1970

Right: Black demonstration in Washington, D.C., Justice Department. Bobby Kennedy speaking to the crowd, June 14, 1963.

tests and viewed on television, strongly help to shape public opinion about the war.

The following are key Civil Rights events occurring during U.S. involvement in Vietnam.

Rosa Parks—On December 1, 1955, a 42-year-old woman named Rosa Parks found a seat on a Montgomery, Alabama, bus after work. Segregation laws at the time stated blacks must sit in designated seats at the back of the bus, and Parks had complied.

When a white man got on the bus and couldn't find a seat in the white section at the front of the bus, the bus driver instructed Parks and three other blacks to give up their seats. Parks refused and was arrested.

As word of her arrest ignited outrage and support, Parks unwittingly became the "mother of the modern-day civil rights movement." Black community leaders formed the Montgomery Improvement Association (MIA) led by Baptist minister Martin Luther King, Jr., a role which would place him front and center in the fight for civil rights. Parks' courage incited the MIA to stage a boycott of the Montgomery bus system. The Montgomery Bus Boycott lasted 381 days. On November 14, 1956, the Supreme Court ruled that segregated seating was unconstitutional.

Little Rock Nine—In 1954, the civil rights movement gained momentum when the United States Supreme Court made segregation illegal in public schools in the case of *Brown v. Board of Education*.

In 1957, Central High School in Little Rock, Arkansas, asked for volunteers from all-black high schools to attend the formerly segregated school. On September 3, 1957, nine black students, called the Little Rock Nine, arrived at Central High School to begin classes.

They were met by the Arkansas National Guard, on order of Governor Orval Faubus, and a screaming, threatening mob. The Little Rock Nine tried again a couple of weeks later and made it inside but had to be removed for their safety when violence ensued.

Finally, President Dwight D. Eisenhower intervened and ordered federal troops to escort the Little Rock Nine to and from classes at Central High. Still, the students faced continual harassment and prejudice. Their efforts, however, brought much-needed attention to the issue of desegregation and fueled protests on both sides of the issue.

Civil Rights Act of 1957—Even though all Americans had gained the right to vote, many southern states made it difficult for blacks. They often required them to take voter literacy tests that were confusing, misleading, and nearly impossible to pass.

Wanting to show a commitment to the civil rights movement and minimize racial tensions in the South, the Eisenhower administration pressured Congress to consider new civil rights legislation.

On September 9, 1957, President Eisenhower signed the Civil Rights Act of 1957 into law, the first major civil rights legislation since Reconstruction. It allowed federal prosecution of anyone who tried to prevent someone from voting. It also created a commission to investigate voter fraud.

Woolworth's Lunch Counter—Despite making some gains, blacks still experienced blatant prejudice in their daily lives. On February 1, 1960, four college students took a stand against segregation in Greensboro, North Carolina, when they refused to leave a Woolworth's lunch counter without being served. Over the next several days, hundreds of people joined their cause in what became known as the Greensboro sit-ins. After some were arrested and charged with trespassing, protestors launched a boycott of all segregated lunch counters.

The owners conceded and the original four students were finally served at the Woolworth's lunch counter where they had first stood their ground. Their efforts spearheaded peaceful sit-ins and demonstrations in dozens of cities and helped launch the Student Nonviolent Coordinating Committee (SNCC) to encourage all students to get involved in the civil rights movement.

This inspired a young college graduate, Stokely Carmichael, who joined SNCC during the Freedom Summer of 1964 to register black voters in Mississippi. In 1966, Carmichael became chair of the SNCC, giving his famous speech, in which he originated the phrase "black power."

Freedom Rider—On May 4, 1961, 13 "Freedom Riders," seven African Americans and six whites, mounted a Greyhound bus in Washington, D.C., embarking on a bus tour of the American South to protest segregated bus terminals. They were testing the 1960 Supreme Court decision *Boynton v. Virginia* declaring segregation of interstate transportation facilities unconstitutional. Facing violence from police and white protesters, they drew international attention.

On Mother's Day 1961, the bus reached Anniston, Alabama, where a mob mounted the bus and threw a bomb into it. The Freedom Riders escaped the burning bus but were severely beaten. Photos of the bus engulfed in flames were widely circulated, and the group could not find a bus driver to take them farther.

U.S. Attorney General Robert Kennedy (brother to President John F. Kennedy) and Alabama Governor John Patterson agreed on a suitable driver, and the Freedom Riders resumed their journey under police escort on May 20. When the officers left the group once they reached Montgomery, a white mob brutally attacked the bus. Attorney General Kennedy responded to the riders and a call from Martin Luther King, Jr., by sending federal marshals to Montgomery.

On May 24, 1961, a group of Freedom Riders reached Jackson, Mississippi. Although met by hundreds of supporters, the group was arrested for trespassing in a "whites-only" facility and sentenced to 30 days in jail. Attorneys for the National Association for the Advancement of Colored People (NAACP) brought the case to the U.S. Supreme Court, who reversed the convictions. Hundreds of Freedom Riders were drawn to the cause, and the rides continued.

In the fall of 1961, pressed by the Kennedy administration, the Interstate Commerce Commission issued regulations prohibiting segregation in interstate transit terminals.

March on Washington—On August 28, 1963, arguably one of the most famous events of the civil rights movement took place—the March on Washington. It was organized and attended by civil rights leaders such as A. Philip Randolph, Bayard Rustin, and Martin Luther King, Jr.

More than 200,000 people, black and white, congregated in Washington, D.C., for the peaceful march intending to force civil rights legislation and establishing job equality for everyone.

Civil Rights March, Wash. DC. 1963.

The highlight of the march was King's speech in which he continually stated, "I have a dream…" which quickly became a slogan for equality and freedom.

Civil Rights Act of 1964—President Lyndon B. Johnson signed the Civil Rights Act of 1964—legislation initiated by

President John F. Kennedy before his assassination—into law on July 2 of that year. King and other civil rights activists witnessed the signing. The law guaranteed equal employment for all, limited the use of voter literacy tests, and allowed federal authorities to ensure public facilities were integrated.

Bloody Sunday—On March 7, 1965, the civil rights movement in Alabama took an especially violent turn as 600 peaceful demonstrators participated in the Selma to Montgomery march to protest the killing of black civil rights activist Jimmie Lee Jackson by a white police officer and to encourage legislation to enforce the 15th amendment. As the protestors neared the Edmund Pettus Bridge, they were blocked by Alabama State Police and local police sent by Alabama governor George C. Wallace, a vocal opponent of desegregation.

Refusing to stand down, protestors moved forward and were viciously beaten and tear-gassed by police, and dozens of protestors were hospitalized. The entire incident was televised and became known as "Bloody Sunday." Some activists wanted to retaliate with violence, but King pushed for nonviolent protests and eventually gained federal protection for another march.

Voting Rights Act of 1965—When President

Johnson signed the Voting Rights Act into law on August 6, 1965, he took the Civil Rights Act of 1964 several steps further. The new law banned all voter literacy tests and provided federal examiners in certain voting jurisdictions. It also allowed the attorney general to contest state and local poll taxes. As a result, poll taxes were later declared unconstitutional in *Harper v. Virginia State Board of Elections* in 1966.

Civil Rights Leaders Assassinated—The civil rights movement had tragic endings for two of its leaders in the late 1960s. On February 21, 1965, former Nation of Islam leader and Organization of Afro-American Unity founder Malcolm X was assassinated at a rally.

On April 4, 1968, civil rights leader and Nobel Peace Prize recipient Martin Luther King, Jr., was assassinated on his hotel room's balcony. Emotionally charged looting and riots followed, putting even more pressure on the Johnson administration to push through additional civil rights laws while U.S. soldiers were in the height of the Vietnam War.

Fair Housing Act of 1968—The Fair Housing Act became law on April 11, 1968, just days after King's assassination. It prevented housing discrimination based on race, sex, national origin, and religion. It was also the last legislation enacted during the civil rights era.

Joe Abodeely

The Civil Rights Movement was an empowering yet precarious time for Blacks in America. The efforts of civil rights activists and countless protestors of all races brought about legislation to end segregation, black voter suppression, and discriminatory employment and housing practices.

The movement also had a negative side to it as civil rights protests involved arsons, thefts, assaults, and the rise of paramilitary groups like the Black Panthers. Martin Luther King, Jr., spoke out against the Vietnam War, falsely claiming that a disproportinate number of Negroes served in Vietnam, which simply was not the truth.

Key Vietnam War Battles

Battle of Ia Drang

Ia Drang was part of the second phase from November 14-18 when the VC launched a conventional attack on U.S. forces that deployed by helicopter close to their main supply bases and the border. In October 1965, the first major battle between U.S. forces (1st Cavalry) and North Vietnam occurred. The VC attacked the Special Forces camp at Plei Me, and the U.S. launched three counterattacks to cut them off from their retreat to Cambodia and destroy them.

In this battle between regular U.S. and North Vietnamese forces, elements of the 1st battalion, 7th Cavalry Regiment, 1st Cavalry Division (Airmobile) fought a pitched battle with Communist main-force units in the Ia Drang Valley of the Central Highlands.

The battalion conducted a heliborne assault into Landing Zone X-Ray near the Chu Pong hills.

Above: US Army Major Bruce Crandall flies his helicopter after discharging a load of infantrymen on a search and destroy mission November 14, 1965. Below: Soldiers with the Army's 1st Cavalry Division disembark a UH-1 Iroquois helicopter.

Around noon, the North Vietnamese 33rd Regiment attacked U.S. troops. The fight continued all day and into the night. American soldiers received support from nearby artillery units and tactical air strikes. The next morning, the North Vietnamese 66th Regiment joined the attack against the U.S. unit. The fighting was bitter, but the tactical air strikes and artillery support took their toll on the enemy and enabled the 1st Cavalry troops to hold on against repeated assaults.

Around noon, more helicopters brought two reinforcing companies to assist the beleaguered soldiers. By the third day of the battle, the Americans had gained the upper hand. The U.S. military estimates that 3,561 NVA were killed and more than 1,000 were wounded during engagements with the 1st Cavalry.

The U.S. Army estimated 305 U.S. killed and 524 U.S. wounded for the 35-day campaign. By Day 5, the Battle of Ia Drang was over. The U.S. Army 1st Cavalry Division reported 1,500 North Vietnamese deaths by body count, an additional 2,000 by estimate, and 304 deaths among their own troops.

In a related action during the same battle, 2nd Battalion, 7th Cavalry, was ambushed by North Vietnamese forces as it moved overland to Landing Zone Albany. Of the 500 men in the original column,

U.S. Army rifle squad of the 1/9 Squadron, 1st Cavalry Division exiting a Huey helicopter in Vietnam.

150 were killed and only 84 were able to return to immediate duty; Company C suffered 93 percent casualties, half of them deaths. Despite these numbers, senior American officials in Saigon declared the Battle of the Ia Drang Valley a great victory.

The battle was extremely important because it was the first significant contact between U.S. troops and North Vietnamese forces. The action demonstrated that the North Vietnamese were prepared to stand and fight major battles even though they might take serious casualties. The battle also demonstrated and

Vietnam Anti-War Movement—the Great American Con Job

U.S. Army Airborne soldiers move through Viet Cong sniper fire toward the jungle after being dropped by Hueys in a rice field, 1967.

validated the value of helicopters for airmobile operations. Senior U.S. military leaders concluded they could wreak significant damage on the Communists in such battles which led to a war of attrition as the U.S. forces tried to wear down the Communists.

Tet Offensive 1968

In April 1967, the North Vietnamese (NVA) began planning their General Offensive and Uprising.

In July 1967, North Vietnam's Communist leaders decided to gamble upon a course of action that would ideally break the stalemate between North Vietnam and U.S.-backed South Vietnam. The intent was to galvanize discontent in the South that would, in turn, force the collapse of the government and army of South Vietnamese leader Nguyen Van Thieu. This offensive could convince the United States that it (the U.S.) could not win the war.

The offensive was preceded by broadcasts from the clandestine "Liberation Radio" network, in which the Alliance of National, Democratic, and Peace Forces, a Viet Cong urban front group, exhorted the South Vietnamese people to rise in open revolt against the Saigon government. Citizens were called on "to side with the ranks of the people and to give their arms and ammunition to the revolutionary armed forces."

By December 1967, U.S. military commanders in Saigon saw there were indications that the Viet Cong and the North Vietnamese were preparing for a major military campaign.

On January 21, 1968, one of their greatest diversions was the attack on the military base at Khe Sanh; but on January 30-31, 1968, during the Tet New Year holiday truce, the NVA launched a surprise attack on over 100 major cities, towns, villages, and most major allied airfields in South Vietnam. Despite advance warnings, the North Vietnamese offensive in the early morning hours of January 30–31 was larger and more intense than U.S. intelligence anticipated.

North Vietnamese forces struck in sudden attacks on urban areas throughout South Vietnam, and briefly held portions of Saigon and 36 of the country's 44 provincial capitals. The NVA captured Hue city on January 31, and U.S. and ARVN troops spent nearly a month in vicious street-to-street fighting taking it back in March. NVA were driven out within two or three days, but some fighting lasted in about five cities. None of the (ARVN) South Vietnamese deserted or defected.

In Saigon, attackers entered both the presidential palace and the compound of the U.S. embassy. North Vietnamese units in Cho Lon, a historic Chinese district west of Saigon, were blasted out in prolonged fighting that demolished large portions of the area. Viet Cong and North Vietnamese troops occupied the walled fortress of Hue, Vietnam's ancient capital, until they were finally driven out by U.S. and South Vietnamese forces on February 24. It was estimated that only 7,000 of Hue's 17,000 homes were left standing after the battle for the city.

The North Vietnamese and Viet Cong paid dearly for their deviation from the guerrilla warfare strategy that had so frustrated U.S. commanders. Initial United States Information Agency estimates placed the number of Communists dead at 60,000 (a figure that was subsequently revised down), with 24,000 weapons captured. The North Vietnamese and Viet Cong had never suffered such casualties before, and the South Vietnamese rejected the North's call to rebellion.

U.S. and South Vietnamese casualties numbered 12,727, including more than 2,600 fatalities. Although U.S. commanders generally held a low opinion of the Army of the Republic of South Vietnam (ARVN), South Vietnamese soldiers fought with bravery and tenacity during the Tet Offensive as shown by the battle for Hue, where ARVN troops and U.S. Marines liberated the city after engaging in some of the fiercest close quarters combat of the war.

The South Vietnamese government reported that 7,721 civilians were killed in the fighting during Tet, while an additional 18,516 were wounded. Throughout the country, some 75,000 homes were damaged or destroyed. More than 670,000 people were declared refugees, raising the total number of internally displaced persons in South Vietnam to some 1.5 million.

The first phase of the Tet Offensive ended by March 28, though fighting at Khe Sanh went into April. The Tet offensive ended on September 23 and was a failure for the NVA. Communist leadership in Hanoi had gambled on a conventional assault that they thought would sweep aside ARVN forces and topple the "puppet" government in Saigon.

NVA and Viet Cong advances were checked by surprisingly resilient ARVN defenders; and most cities, with the notable exception of Hue, were liberated within days of the initial attack. In addition, the widespread loss of life and destruction of property triggered a decline in support for the Viet Cong among the South Vietnamese populace.

U.S. and South Vietnamese officials declared that the Communists had suffered a resounding military defeat, and this was certainly true, but Walter Cronkite portrayed Tet as a victory for the Communists. Why did he do that?

Battle of Hue—Tet 1968

The Battle for Hue, Tet 1968, was the attack on the old Imperial capital of Hue by forces of the North Vietnamese Army and South Vietnamese insurgents of the National Liberation Front during the Tet Offensive.

A division-size force of North Vietnamese Army and Viet Cong soldiers launched a well-coordinated multi-pronged attack on the city. Their strategic objective was to "liberate" the entire city, but it failed totally as its occupants were solidly on the side of the American and South Vietnamese. With a wartime population of about 140,000 persons, Hue retained much of its pre-war ambience. It had been immune to much of the war. Unknown to the allies, enemy regiments were on the move toward Hue. The 6th NVA had as its three primary objectives—the *Mang Ca* headquarters compound, the Tay Loc airfield, and the Imperial palace, all in the Citadel. South of the Perfume River, the 4th NVA was to attack the modern city.

The Communist forces hoped a popular uprising by the "oppressed" people in South Vietnam would lead to a general uprising and overthrow of the "puppet" regime supported by the United States. Hue was the only city to be completely occupied by the Communist forces during the massive offensive and was the scene of violent and close quarter fighting that raged for nearly a month, from January 31 to February 25, 1968.

The NVA attack began early on January 31, and by 0800, North Vietnamese troops raised the red and blue Viet Cong banner with its gold star over the Citadel flag tower. It was quite a shock to the allies. It was not until February 24, that the U.S. Marines finally prevailed and had retaken the Citadel and NVA flag.

The U.S. Marines, not being well trained in urban combat found a harrowing house-to-house, booby-trap-infested ordeal as they swept through every inch of the city. Since it was monsoon season, it was virtually impossible for the U.S. forces to use air support. Armor and airstrikes were extremely limited to the conditions, and to keep casualties down, the Allied forces were ordered not to bomb or shell the city, for fear of destroying the historic structures.

But as the intensity of the battle increased, the policy was eliminated. The Communist forces were constantly using snipers, hidden inside buildings or in small holes, and prepared makeshift machine gun bunkers.

The Communists suffered heavy losses in this battle, losing 5,133 men at Hue; about 3,000 more were estimated to be killed outside of the city. Basically, the whole attack force was wiped out. Approximately 2,800 people were killed by the NVA and VC simply because they were pro-allied. Mass graves of executed and other atrocities were unearthed. American losses were 142.

An interesting and little-mentioned aspect to the

After the recapture of Hue in 1968, several mass graves were discovered. Many had been clubbed, shot, or simply buried alive. As many as 2,800 South Vietnamese civilians were executed.

Battle of Hue was the use of fire team assault boats by the Marines. A fire team assault boat platoon consisted of 12 boats. Each boat was 16 feet long, made of fiberglass, had a 50 hp Mercury motor, four men, and a mounted M-60 machine gun. These assault boats were used primarily for river operations—patrolling the waterways—but some of them acted as waterborne infantry at the heavily defended East Gate of the Citadel. They transported wounded across the Perfume River and conducted search and destroy missions.

Vietnam Anti-War Movement—the Great American Con Job

Marines' tanks and ARVNs traversed a wall and were moving toward the city when they were ordered not to take it for political reasons because ARVNs were to take back the city of Hue.

The 26-day effort by the U.S. Marines, U.S. Army, and ARVN to recapture the Citadel produced a stunning military defeat for the Communists.

Yet, the strategic victory ultimately went to the Communists because the scenes of bloody fighting via TV in Hue, Saigon, and other cities in Vietnam during the Tet offensive so shocked the American people that the pressure to withdraw from the war was overwhelming.

Vietnam was the first ever American televised war with nightly news coverage; people watched the blood and napalm as they ate their dinner. The draft in America was immensely unpopular, with many college age men burning their draft cards, heading to Canada, or claiming to be a drug addict or homosexual to get out of serving.

Not all Americans were against the war, but the Battle of Hue and the Tet Offensive of 1968 was the turning point, and Walter Cronkite, the most trusted man in America, contributed to it.

Joe Abodeely

Battle of Firebase Ripcord

From March 12 to July 23, 1970, the Battle of Fire Support Base Ripcord was a four-month long battle between elements of the U.S. Army 101st Airborne Division and two reinforced divisions of the North Vietnamese Army. Attempting to retake the initiative, the 101st was to rebuild the abandoned Fire Support Base Ripcord in the A Shau Valley. They relied heavily on the helicopters for support in the difficult terrain as the 101st Airborne became an air assault division.

The firebase was set on four hilltops as outposts for a planned offensive by the Marines to search and destroy the NVA supply lines in the mountains overlooking the A Shau valley.

As the 101st soldiers rebuilt the base and prepared the attack on the enemy supply lines, the NVA launched sporadic attacks from March 12 until June 30. It is estimated that as much as 25,000 NVA troops were then positioned in the A Shau Valley area at the time.

On the morning of July 1, 1970, the NVA started firing mortars and besieged the firebase for 23 days; 75 U.S. servicemen were killed. The battle for the hilltops raged for days. Surrounded and outnumbered almost ten to one and running low on supplies, the 101st held out and kept the enemy from overrunning the firebase. It was the last major confrontation between U.S. ground forces and North Vietnam in the war. The final death toll was 138 American soldiers and 3 men missing in action.

Easter Offensive

The 1972 Spring-Summer Offensive or the Easter Offensive, was conducted by the NVA (the regular army of North Vietnam) against the ARVN (the regular army of South Vietnam) and the United States military between March 30 and October 22, 1972. The U.S. high command expected an attack in 1972, but the size and ferocity of the assault stunned the defenders because the attackers struck on three fronts simultaneously, with the bulk of the NVA.

This first attempt by the NVA to invade the south since Tet 1968 was characterized by conventional infantry-armor assaults backed by heavy artillery with both sides using the latest technological advances in weapons systems. The NVA major offensive in the South on March 30 included 40,000 NVA troops and over 600 armored vehicles and tanks crossing the border from the North and Cambodia.

It was the largest offensive operation since 300,000 Chinese troops had crossed the Yalu River into North Korea during that war, and the Communists seized the cities of Quang Tri, Hue, An Loc, and Kon Tum. The U.S. responded by carpet bombing the North; and though South Vietnam recaptured Quang Tri, it lost 10% of its land to the North.

Fighting ended on October 22; North Vietnam was repelled; but they kept their newly occupied territory and got their bargaining chip. In the I Corps Tactical Zone, NVA forces overran South Vietnamese defensive positions in a month-long battle and captured Quang Tri city, before attempting to seize Hue.

NVA similarly eliminated frontier defense forces in the II Corps Tactical Zone and seized the provincial capital of Kon Tum, threatening to open a way to the sea, which would have split South Vietnam in two. Northeast of Saigon, in the III Corps Tactical Zone, NVA forces overran Loc Ninh and advanced to assault the capital of Bình Long Province at An Loc.

The campaign was in three phases: April was a month of NVA advances; May became a period of equilibrium; in June and July the ARVN counterattacked, recapturing Quang Tri City in September. Initial North Vietnamese successes were hampered by high casualties, inept tactics, and the increasing application of U.S. and South Vietnamese air power. The offensive was not designed to win the war outright but to gain as much territory and destroy as many units of the ARVN as possible, to improve the North's negotiating position as the Paris Peace Accords were concluding.

A result of the offensive was U.S. launching of Operation Linebacker II, the first sustained bombing of North Vietnam by the U.S. since November 1968. The ARVN troops fought bravely and repulsed and drove the NVA back.

The Vietnamization proved successful. Nixon did not send in U.S. ground troops during the invasion, and he continued the final withdraw of the last U.S. combat troops that year. Despite post-war characterizations, the ARVN troops proved they could stand up to the NVA. The combination of the bombing of the rail lines in the North, the mining of harbors, and the "December bombing" campaign put North Vietnam at a severe disadvantage.

Although ARVN (South Vietnamese forces) withstood their greatest trial thus far in the conflict, the NVA gained valuable territory within South Vietnam from which to launch future offensives and they obtained a better bargaining position at the peace negotiations being conducted in Paris.

Paris Peace Accords

President Nixon wanted "peace with honor," so he bombed Haiphong and Hanoi between March 30 and October 22, 1972, and ultimately ended U.S. action in the war. The NVA leaders were surprised when the U.S. halted the bombing campaign in January and later admitted they were at their breaking point. The 1972 Easter Offensive was conducted by the NVA against the ARVN and the United States military. Nixon knew the new Congress would not be favorable to him regarding the war, and he wanted a deal before they were to take office. South Vietnam was forced to agree to a deal they did not like only to appease both the President and Congress.

On January 27, 1973, the Paris Peace Accords were signed, ending the Vietnam War. The treaty specified that U.S. forces and Communist forces were to leave South Vietnam at that time, but the U.S. could send war material to South Vietnam if NVA and VC renewed hostile actions. U.S. POWs were to be returned, and the vast majority of U.S. forces left Vietnam.

In June 1973, the Case-Church Amendment, prohibited further U.S. military activity in Vietnam, unless the President got Congressional approval in advance, and ended direct U.S. military involvement in the Vietnam War.

Congress stopped support of war materials to South Vietnamese forces as the NVA resumed attacks. The Case-Church Amendment sealed the fate of South Vietnam and the entire region because the reduction of support and aid to South Vietnam prevented them from defending themselves with the promised equipment and financial aid per the Paris Peace Accords.

After U.S. troops left, North Vietnamese Army and Viet Cong continued to invade cities in South Vietnam in violation of the Peace Accords. Nixon wanted "peace with honor"; Democrats wanted to get Nixon. In 1974, the Watergate issue forced Nixon to resign. On April 9, 1975, they entered Dong Nai Province, the final swath which led to Saigon. Thousands of South Vietnamese sought refuge elsewhere and left Vietnam as the "boat people."

North Vietnamese Army and Viet Cong troops captured Saigon in April 1975, two years after U.S. forces left. The anti-war crowd rejoiced as NVA tanks entered the Saigon palace grounds.

Battle of Xuan Loc

The U.S. Congress did not fulfill its promise to help South Vietnam under SEATO or the Peace Accords when the NVA invaded them again in 1973. Congress refused to fund the war material. As previously noted, the Case-Church Amendment sealed the fate of South Vietnam and the entire region. Although most units fought valiantly, South Vietnamese forces ran out of ammo, fuel, and equipment to fight as the NVA intensified its invasion of South Vietnam.

Before U.S. forces left Vietnam in 1973, the ARVN (South Vietnamese) had developed into a force which could defend itself if the U.S. continued supplying arms and equipment, but in the Central Highlands, South Vietnam's II Corps was completely destroyed while attempting to evacuate to the Mekong Delta region. In the cities of Hue and Da Nang, ARVN units simply dissolved without putting up resistance.

The Battle of Xuan Loc was unique in many respects for the Vietnam War, involving units of divisional size, devastatingly effective Viet Nam Air Force (VNAF) airpower, and sophisticated U.S.-made Daisy Cutter Bombs. It was the last major battle of the Vietnam War.

From the beginning of 1975, the NVA forces swept through the northern provinces of South Vietnam virtually unopposed. The ARVN committed almost all their remaining mobile forces, especially the 18th Division, under Brigadier General Lê Minh Đảo, to the defense of the strategic crossroads town of Xuan Loc, hoping to stall the NVA advance.

Brigadier General Lê Minh Đảo

The 18th Division lodged themselves in the town of Xuan Loc and were able to block North Vietnam's advance for nearly two weeks. The ARVN held Xuan Loc and counterattacked against impossible odds and fought well at Xuan Loc. It was described as "heroic and gallant" by the South Vietnamese defenders and as one of the few places where the ARVN, though outnumbered, stood and fought with a tenacity which stunned their opponents. The stand of the ARVN so impressed the rest of the entire South Vietnamese Army, that previously routed, they grew confident again.

After 12 days and nights of ferocious combat against the North Vietnamese Communist forces, the steel defensive line at Xuan Loc (Long Khanh) still held firm. The fighting was harsh and severe, but the ARVN troops held up the assault on Saigon for two weeks. Xuan Loc was reduced to rubble in the fight, and its population fled in a mass exodus. North Vietnamese 4th Corps forces engaged in the battle had suffered heavy losses; therefore, the Headquarters of the Ho Chi Minh Campaign hastily changed their plan for the attack on Saigon. The forces of the North Vietnamese 3rd Corps in Tay Ninh and 2nd Corps at the Nuoc Trong base would be used to make the "major effort" to attack and capture Saigon. The NVA 4th Corps abandoned its efforts against Xuan Loc and became a "reserve force."

Xuan Loc was no longer a "hot point," and the Headquarters of ARVN 3rd Corps/Military Region 3 ordered the 18th Infantry Division and all units participating in the Xuan Loc (Long Khanh) battle to retreat to Bien Hoa on April 20, 1975, to establish a new line defending the outer approaches to Saigon.

This withdrawal marked the end of Thieu's political career, as he resigned on April 21, 1975. After Xuan Loc fell on April 21, 1975, the NVA battled with the last remaining elements of III Corps Armored Task Force, remnants of the 18th Infantry Division, and depleted Marine, Airborne, and Ranger Battalions in a fighting retreat that lasted nine days, until they reached Saigon. The North Vietnamese broke through Xuan Loc with Soviet T54 tanks and headed straight toward Bien Hoa and arrived at Saigon at the end of the month.

The Fall of Saigon

On April 9, 1975, NVA entered Dong Nai Province, the final swath which led to Saigon. Thousands of South Vietnamese sought refuge elsewhere and left Vietnam as the "boat people."

When Xuan Loc fell on April 21, all order collapsed. Hoping to find safety in American-held Saigon, the ARVN and South Vietnam civilians made a chaotic retreat from the advancing North Vietnamese.

Xuan Loc was only 26 miles away from Saigon, so the Communists were already at their doorstep. By

April 27, 1975, Saigon was surrounded. On April 29, the shelling began, and the following day, the NVA entered the capital.

The orderly evacuation of Americans and South Vietnam civilians turned into chaos. NVA armored columns crashed through the gates of South Vietnam's Presidential Palace, and U.S. military involvement in the Vietnam War finally ended on April 30, 1975.

Ultimately, estimates of the number of Vietnamese soldiers and civilians killed vary from 966,000 to 3,812,000. Current 2017 records report that the conflict resulted in 58,318 U.S. fatalities. And then there were the "boat people" and the "reeducation camps."

Mayaguez Incident

On May 12, 1975, Cambodian Navy gunboats seized the American merchant ship, *SS Mayaguez*, in international waters off Cambodia's coast.

The ship was being towed toward the Cambodian mainland when word reached the White House. President Ford was determined that the situation not be allowed to deteriorate into another drawn-out *Pueblo* incident. In addition, it was believed important to counter a growing perception among U.S. friends and adversaries that America was "a helpless giant" and an erratic ally lacking determination.

The U.S. response to the seizure would be a military operation executed by an *ad hoc* force of airmen, Marines, and sailors. The U.S. had no diplomatic relations with the Khmer Rouge, which had taken control of Cambodia in previous weeks. U.S. forces stationed in neighboring Thailand were numerically insufficient for ground action against Cambodia, and no U.S. warships were in the district.

Time was a compelling factor. The big concern was that the Cambodians would transfer the crew to the mainland, making the rescue operation more arduous. For those in authority to make an enlightened decision, it was necessary that more than one plan be considered. According to then Chief of Staff General David C. Jones, five plans were prepared. Option Four, a twin-pronged marine assault coupled with the bombing of selected targets, was Ford's choice. In such situations as hostage rescue attempts, planning is usually based on assumptions or speculation, especially during the first hours or days of the crisis. Intelligence data were sufficient for an operation with all its possibilities. Within a few minutes of receiving the mayday message sent by the *Mayaguez*, a Ready Alert Bird was airborne.

By 10:30 p.m., the first report on the *Mayaguez* was received at Cubi Point Naval Air Station. It was too dark for Ready Alert Bird and its crew to eyeball the ship, but they could see a captured merchant vessel on their radar screens as a big image flanked by two little images. Option Four was an extravagant scheme that employed two destroyers, one aircraft carrier, two Marine units with 12 helicopters, and a generous complement of Air Force fighters, bombers, and reconnaissance aircraft. President Ford believed strongly that it was better to use too much force than too little.

Ford ordered the aircraft carrier *Coral Sea* and other navy ships to proceed at full speed to the Gulf of Thailand, as well as planes in the Philippines to locate the *Mayaguez* and keep it in view. A Navy P-3 located the ship anchored off Koh-Tang Island, 40 miles from Cambodia. Several observance aircraft were damaged by gunfire from the island. A battalion-sized Marine rescue team was airlifted from Okinawa to U-Tapao Airforce Base in the Gulf of Thailand, about 300 miles from Koh-Tang.

The destroyer *USS Holt* was directed to seize the *Mayaguez*, while Marines, airlifted and supported by the Air Force, would rescue the crew, at least some of whom were believed to be held on Koh-Tang.

Concurrently, the Coral Sea would launch four bombing strikes on military targets near Kompong Som to convince the Khmer Rouge that the U.S. was serious.

Expecting only light resistance, the U.S. troops were met by a force of 150 to 200 heavily armed Khmer Rouge soldiers who shot down three of the first eight helicopters and damaged two others. About 100 Marines were put ashore, but it soon became clear that substantial reinforcements would be needed. The assault force was supported by Air Force planes, but the attack was not going well.

While the firefight on Koh-Tang was at its most intense, bombing targets on the mainland apparently convinced the Khmer Rouge leaders that they had underestimated U.S. resolve. A fishing boat was seen to approach the destroyer *Wilson* with white flags flying, and the 39 crewmen of the *Mayaguez* were aboard.

The Marines on Koh-Tang were ordered to disengage and withdraw, but Khmer Rouge troops continued the battle, taking the offensive as Air Force helicopters moved through heavy fire to withdraw U.S. forces. The last of 230 Marines were not evacuated until after dark on the night of May 15. As they had throughout the Vietnam War, helicopter crews performed with unsurpassed heroism. Eighteen Marines and airmen were killed or missing in the assault and withdrawal from Koh-Tang. Twenty-three others were killed in a helicopter crash in route from Nakhon Phanom to U-Tapao, but the objectives of the operation were achieved. The *Mayaguez* and its crew had been rescued, though at high cost.

Firefight Near Hue

The North Vietnamese Army (NVA) captured portions of Hue Citadel, and their intent was to "liberate" the entire city as part of a countrywide popular uprising to sweep the Viet Cong into power. They failed due to U.S. military action. The people of Hue and others in Vietnam turned their backs on the Communists during

Citadel at Hue

the Tet Offensive. The Communists who seized and occupied Hue committed atrocities on the civilian populace. They murdered over 5800 civilians—hands tied behind their backs, chained together and killed by the Communists. Politicians, policemen, military, farmers, women, young girls, and children were executed.

The ensuing 26-day effort by the U.S. Marines, U.S. Army, and South Viet Nam Army (ARVN) to recapture the Citadel produced a stunning military defeat for the invaders, but the U.S. media grossly misrepresented this fact.

A group of armed Vietnamese military and their tank, 1968.

Vietnam Anti-War Movement—the Great American Con Job

Above: Eight inch (203 mm) M110 self-propelled Howitzer. Below: Armored Personnel Carrier (APC) patrolling a defensive perimeter.

Joe Abodeely

A Marine observation plane makes a low level pass over Hue during action in the Imperial City.

The "strategic victory" during Tet ultimately went to the Communists because the media led by Walter Cronkite misinformed the American public about the U.S. success at Hue and The Citadel at Hue.

The Tet Offensive of 1968 began on January 31, 1968. Major cities, towns, and installations such as Saigon, Hue, and Khe Sanh were subjected to violent attacks by the Viet Cong and the North Vietnamese Army (NVA) with the intent to incite a major uprising by the Vietnamese people against their American protectors. Contrary to what Walter Cronkite and other

Vietnam Anti-War Movement—the Great American Con Job

1st Cavalry Division helicopter resupply mission northwest of Hue, February, 1968.

media purveyors of prevarication said to the public, the offensive was a disastrous military failure.

In the later part of February 1968, I was an infantry lieutenant, second platoon leader of Delta Company of the 2nd battalion 7th Cavalry of the 3rd brigade of the 1st Cavalry Division (airmobile). On February 21, during the rainy season, I flew from Camp Evans to near an old French compound (maybe a convent or monastery) between Hue and the DMZ to defend 8-inch guns (8-inch diameter shells) and 175 mm artillery batteries which were providing fire support to the Marines and some 1st Cav units fighting at Hue, the walled imperial city with much beauty and great history, the ancient Imperial Capital of Vietnam.

I think we were only around 25 "clicks" (kilometers) from Hue, which had suffered intense fighting. We were right near Highway 1 on the main supply line to Hue and had set up a defensive perimeter with the artillery.

On Sunday, February 25, the day after the ARVN troops pulled down the Viet Cong flag flying over the Citadel at Hue, Delta Company HQ, 1st Platoon and 2nd Platoon (mine), swept the nearby area around the old French compound about 7 to 10 miles northwest of Hue. We moved in a column formation through the villages looking for VC and NVA troops.

My platoon was on point and was fired on several times that day. The sniper shots came close because we could hear the crack of the bullets as they broke the sound barrier or the twang as they went by. The monsoon season was miserable as we hiked in mud and high humidity.

We conducted "sweeps" through jungle, on the sand along the coast, crossed streams and rice paddies, and searched villages—the houses, hooches, or huts. We looked for VC, NVA, weapons, or rice caches, which were their food supply. In highly vegetated areas, my platoon moved along in a column, or single file, or a modified column, which was an oval-looking formation, if the terrain allowed.

When we crossed open areas, rice paddies or along the sand, or if we were in an assault phase, I put the platoon "online"—a straight lateral line with weapons forward for maximum firepower. Our weapons were always "at the ready." Many of us took a hand grenade ring from the pin, attached it to the front rifle sight of our M-16s, and tied a nylon cord or shoelace to that ring and to the stock's rear.

We slung the improvised sling over our shoulders and had our shooting hand on the pistol grip of the rifle and our thumb on the selector switch of the rifle ready to flick it from "safety" to "semi" to "auto." But my main job was to lead and direct my platoon, not to fire my M-16. I did love the M-16 and qualified "expert" with it.

Occasionally, we heard the artillery at the base pounding out fire missions directed in support of units at Hue. These big guns supported them. The Marines and a couple of units of the 1st Cav saw hell in the battle of Hue, which probably explains why Walter Cronkite, after talking to Marines, changed his original report about how well U.S. troops did at Hue to a pessimistic view that maybe the U.S should call it a draw and go home. But the Marines did a great job in liberating Hue.

On February 27, my company commander called me over to his C.P. and said "Skeeter" (as he called me and as we looked at a map), "I want you to take your platoon and go north along the river." We were hoping to "make contact" with the enemy.

Patrolling was serious business because we left the security of a base camp. I got my platoon ready—we checked our weapons, ammo, smoke and fragmentation grenades, gear, radios and SOI (signal operating instructions), and C-rations. We walked out of the base camp perimeter and proceeded on our mission.

It had been raining for days, but the sun was out this day. My platoon moved along in relatively open areas in a modified squad column for ease of movement, control, and security. I formed the platoon into three squads—each with a PRC-25 radio, and I had two RTOs (radio/telephone operators) with PRC-25s at my side for constant communication. When we got into jungle, we went into single file with troops posted as flank security, and I positioned my RTOs and me behind the lead squad for the best command and control and reaction capability.

We came to a village, which was deserted except

for an old man who had his nose cut off. His face had a triangle scar where his nose should be (like the triangle cut in a Halloween pumpkin). He told us that there were no VC (Viet Cong) in the area. Sergeant Duk (pronounced Duke), an ARVN interpreter along with us, did the questioning; and neither Duk nor I believed this guy. We left him and moved through the empty village. It was ominous that no one else was around.

As we moved along on our patrol, we were still moving in a platoon column formation with my two RTOs and me positioned behind the lead squad. I heard "small-arms" fire up in front of my lead squad. Since we all had stopped to eat lunch (our C-rations), I checked to see what was happening up front.

My point man told me that he saw what appeared to be an ARVN who fired at him. The ARVNs were the soldiers of the Republic of South Viet Nam—the people we were there to protect from the Communist NVA (who invaded from the north) and the Viet Cong who were insurgents and "terrorists" to the people and government of South Viet Nam. The soldier said he shot at the ARVN, and he thought he hit him. He thought the guy was an ARVN because he was wearing green fatigues. Whoever this guy was, he wasn't friendly.

We moved to a small ditch and saw some blood,

which indicated that the "ARVN" had been hit. At about the same time, a small "bubble" chopper flew overhead nearby, and we heard automatic weapons fire apparently directed at the chopper. I did not want to pursue the "ARVN" who we thought did the firing at the chopper because it looked like he was leading us away from proceeding along the river as we were heading north.

We ignored his firing as we continued along the river. Finally, we got to a road, which went over a small wooden bridge over a small stream. There were trees and other thick foliage around the bridge and stream. The platoon carefully and quickly crossed the bridge and assembled behind and around an abandoned stone house surrounded with trees and other vegetation. On the side of the house opposite our location was an open rice paddy clearing with a tree line and stone buildings approximately a couple hundred meters away.

The point man came back to my location and said, "2-6, I just saw about twelve or thirteen NVA moving along in a trench" off to our left front. "2-6" was my call sign and nickname. The "2" meant second platoon, and the "6" meant leader. He assured me they were NVA because of their khaki uniforms and pith helmets.

I immediately tried to get everyone assembled in a good defensive position around the house because we weren't dug in and were extremely vulnerable. All of a sudden, all hell broke loose! RPG (rocket propelled grenade) rounds started coming in, exploding on the other side of the stone house. Automatic weapons fire seemed to come continuously from our left front, front, and right front. Bullets were popping by us no matter where we moved. The point man and his backup point man were returning fire, but they were out in the open.

I saw the point man lying in a prone position pumping out a lot of rounds from his M-16, and I saw a bullet hit his steel pot (helmet) and throw sparks as it glanced off. His backup point man stood up behind him and fired several rounds. Suddenly, the standing backup point man got hit in the arm and in the torso and went down.

Some of us were able to get into one of the NVA trenches near our position for cover; and as the bullets were coming from everywhere, we expended a lot of ammo in return fire. A firefight is sheer pandemonium—automatic weapons fire, *dut-dut-dut-dut-dut-dut,* and the snapping or popping of incoming small-arms fire, the explosions coming in (rocket propelled grenades), and going out (our 90 mm recoilless rifle) is an experience very difficult for me to explain.

A blond kid we called "Smitty" was firing his M-60 machine gun from an old leafless tree. He was standing up behind the tree making the machine gun spew forth its rain of steel as fast as the metal links of the ammunition belt would allow without jamming the gun. Since he was not behind cover, he took a round clean through his arm. We got him to our location in the trench, gave him morphine, and he slept throughout the rest of the firefight.

My platoon sergeant, medic, and I crawled out of the trench under heavy enemy fire (bullets "popping" everywhere) and dragged the wounded soldier (the backup point man) back to the trench. He was gurgling; he had been shot in the arm, spun around, and shot in the lung. I found out later that he got transported to Tokyo and lived. I now had five men wounded—three were hit with the first in-coming RPG rounds.

My artillery forward observer who came along with us was trying desperately to get some artillery support for us. He kept calling on his radio for artillery, but all the guns were trained on Hue because there was a lot of action going on there, so we couldn't get artillery. I had a firestorm to contend with. We were completely surrounded by a much larger and entrenched force; I had wounded men; and we could not get artillery support. Things were not good.

At one point we tried to see if we could get back

across the bridge. I asked a young sergeant to take a few men to see if they could cross the bridge. He said, "Sir, we'll get killed if we go out there." As scared as I was, I knew I was going to have to lead a few men to check out a withdrawal route.

I took my RTO (radio/telephone operator) and a few other men, and we slowly eased out of the NVA trench and low-crawled to a furrowed field. Bullets were still flying everywhere as we hugged the earth for dear life. As our mini "patrol" eased back toward the little wooden bridge, two snipers in trees at the bridge started firing at us. They pinned us down, and we couldn't move.

My RTO was able to get us an ARA (aerial rocket artillery helicopter gunship). It was a Huey armed with rocket pods and two M-60 door-gunners. We were the 1st Air Cav, so we had the lift ships to haul troops and logistics; and we had the gunships—the ARAs on call. The snipers kept us pinned down, so we lay flat in the furrows of the field. I could hear the snap of the bullets breaking the sound barrier as they passed by. We hugged those furrows for dear life.

We directed the ARA to fire on the trees with the snipers, and the helicopter made a couple of passes firing rockets. The screaming hiss of the rockets, which seemed to go right over our heads, convinced me we would be hit by "friendly fire." I just knew they would hit us—but they didn't. The gunship did a good job of hitting where we told him, but the snipers were still there. We crawled back to the trench after the unsuccessful attempt to get back across the bridge.

The firefight continued; at one point, we called in a couple medivac choppers for our wounded. Prior to their arrival, my platoon sergeant, and I used machetes to try to clear a LZ (landing zone) so they could land. We got out from our cover, stood up, and hacked at saplings and brush; we made a suitable LZ to pick up our wounded. For some mysterious reason, the NVA firing lightened up as we were clearing the area.

As the medivac helicopters descended and then landed, the NVA quit firing. We loaded the five wounded troopers on the choppers, and they took off. After the medivac choppers were in the air, out of the fighting, and on their way to save lives, the firing started up again. To this day, I don't know why the NVA stopped shooting when they did, but I'd like to think they recognized the big Red Cross on the front of the medivac ships and honored the Geneva Conventions.

While all of these events were occurring, we of course notified Heavy Bones 6 (my CO), who was bringing the first and third and mortar platoons up to give us some support. It seemed to take forever for them to get to our location, but the jungle was thick, and they did not know exactly where we were. Finding something in the thick jungle is like finding a needle in a haystack. Trite, but true.

Prior to the rest of the company's arrival, we were able to get some "4-Deuce" fire support. I never really appreciated the effectiveness of the 4.2-inch mortar until that day. When those 4.2-inch mortar rounds were called in, the shells came crashing down in the open rice paddy and tree line in front of us. The explosions were tremendous—trees were flying, smoke was rising—the *thump-thump, thump-thump* was rhythmic. A 4.2-inch round is like a 105 mm howitzer round but it is 106.6 mm; so, we finally got our artillery after all—from a huge mortar.

As the CO (Heavy Bones 6) got closer to our location, he tried to pinpoint where we were. We generally guided him to our location over the radio, but it was difficult for the rest of the company to know where we were because we had traveled through some jungle; and now, we were taking cover in NVA trenches. To make matters even worse, first platoon was "reconning by fire" as they were approaching us from our right rear. They were shooting randomly into the jungle to secure their path of approach.

Now, we had to worry about getting hit by our own guys. We stayed low, and eventually Delta Company got to the tree line to the right of the NVA as we observed them. My platoon laid down a base of fire as the company minus (the other two rifle platoons and the mortar platoon minus my platoon) acted as the maneuver force. We let loose with our M-16s, M-60s, and M-79s.

After the company swept through the enemy positions, we regrouped south of the wooden bridge. The company had run into what was estimated to be an NVA company or regimental headquarters based on the weapons, communications, and equipment found. It was right on the direct supply line to Hue. Some of the guys told me that there was commo wire all over the place, indicating a major headquarters. The Cav troopers killed an NVA officer, and one of them got his 9 mm pistol as a souvenir.

We had to get a good distance away from the target area to call in an air strike to level the whole area. I think we had moved about a click (1,000 meters) away when a jet roared in and dropped its thunderous payload. We were in a prone position on the ground when the explosion occurred and the ground shook. It was extremely loud. After the blast, I heard this whirling-buzzing sound heading my way. Then a "plop"! About two feet from my leg was a 6-inch by 5-inch chunk of metal fragment from the bomb still smoldering in the dirt.

My CO and the mortar platoon leader said I did a really good job that day. I had five guys wounded; none killed. It was that day that I made up my mind I would not lose any of my men if I could help it. By the end of my tour, I had kept my promise.

I recommended a Silver Star for my point man, and he got it. Other decorations were also awarded—none to me. I heard I was put in for a Silver Star, but the executive officer in the rear nixed it. I think he resented me because of my education, and he was OCS (officer candidate school graduate) without a college degree.

I got the satisfaction that I led my men the way an infantry officer is supposed to lead, but more importantly, I kept them all alive. The survival instinct and my training as a combat infantry unit commander served me well.

The day had been terrifying, exhilarating, challenging, ultrastressful, and emotionally draining, but I learned a lot about the meaning of life, infantry tactics, and myself from that experience. After the mortar platoon leader complimented me, I went over behind a big tree so nobody could see me and cried. I just let out everything I was holding in.

While my whole company, my platoon, and I were experiencing what I just described on February 27, 1968, Walter Cronkite gave the most misleading and devastating media broadcast—*"We Are Mired in Stalemate"* on February 27, 1968:

"...Who won and who lost in the great Tet offensive against the cities? I'm not sure. The Vietcong did not win by a knockout, but neither did we. The referees of history may make it a draw... Khe Sanh could well fall, with a terrible loss in American lives, prestige, and morale, and this is a tragedy of our stubbornness there; but the bastion no longer is a key to the rest of the northern regions, and it is doubtful that the American forces can be defeated across the breadth of the DMZ with any substantial loss of ground. Another standoff...

To say that we are mired in stalemate seems the only realistic, yet unsatisfactory, conclusion... But it is increasingly clear to this reporter that the only rational way out then will be to negotiate, not as victors, but as an honorable people who lived up to their pledge to defend democracy and did the best they could."

The End Of The Siege At Khe Sanh Combat Base

Prelude to the Relief of Khe Sanh

General Westmoreland and the Marines who manned Khe Sanh carried out a campaign to block North Vietnamese infiltration into South Vietnam by way of the Demilitarized Zone that divided the two Vietnams. They also built up a base area which served as a jumping-off point for an American advance into the panhandle region of Laos to cut off the Ho Chi Minh Trail.

The Khe Sanh base was located about fifteen miles south of the Demilitarized Zone and about seven miles from the eastern border of Laos. It was surrounded by towering ridges and was in the center corridors leading through the mountains to the north and northwest of the base.

Khe Sanh overlooked Highway 9 to the south, the only east-west road in the Northern Province to join Laos and the coastal regions. The base was laid out on a flat laterite plateau. It was shaped somewhat like an irregular rectangle and covered an area approximately one mile long and one-half mile wide.

A key feature of the base was a 3,900-foot aluminum mat runway. The nearby Special Forces Camp at Lang Vei was overrun, and aerial resupply of the Combat Base was endangered by intense shelling. This forced the Air Force to drop pallets with supplies from the cargo aircraft skimming the runway without landing (LAPE—Low Altitude Parachute Extraction).

The siege of 6,000 Marines at Khe Sanh who were surrounded by 20,000 North Vietnamese troops began on January 21, 1968. Its location in northwest

Khe Sanh Combat Base and Air Strip.

South Vietnam was vital because it was a base for allied operations to block five avenues of Communist infiltration of men and supplies from Laos into South Vietnam.

If Khe Sanh were abandoned, entire North Vietnamese divisions could pour down Route 9 (the major east-west highway below the DMZ) and four other natural approaches through the valleys and overrun a chain of Marine positions—the Rockpile, Con Thien, Dong Ha, and Phu Bai to the east. The North Vietnamese could seize control of South Vietnam's two northernmost provinces, Quang Tri and Thua Thien-Hue, with severe political and psychological consequences.

Since January 22, 1968, allied airmen had dropped 80,000 tons of ordnance around Khe Sanh, more than the nonnuclear tonnage dropped on Japan throughout World War II, but the bombing had limited effectiveness. It had not stopped enemy movement around Khe Sanh.

On February 6 and 7, using amphibious light tanks, the NVA attacked Lang Vei Special Forces camp located 7 kilometers (4.3 miles) from Khe Sanh. Two Marine companies at Khe Sanh could not execute a preplanned rescue only 4 miles outside the wire because the NVA controlled Route 9, and the NVA were deadly.

On February 8, NVA gunners fired hundreds of mortar rounds into a Marine position on nearby Hill 64, followed by an assault that resulted in 21 men killed, 26 wounded, and four Marines missing in action. During the previous week, the NVA managed to fire 1,500 rocket, artillery, and mortar rounds at the Khe Sanh Base.

On February 25, a Marine two-squad patrol, which was instructed not to venture farther than 1,000 meters from the base perimeter, vanished. Two weeks later, casualties of the so-called "ghost patrol" were established as nine dead, 25 wounded, and 19 missing. On March 25, a Marine patrol was halted by heavy enemy machine gun and mortar fire after traveling only 100 to 200 yards past the camp's barbed wire perimeter. On March 30, a company-size patrol had as one of its missions the recovery of the bodies of the ghost patrol. This second patrol suffered three dead, 71 wounded, and three missing before being ordered to pull back. Only two bodies from the ghost patrol were recovered at that time. Lieutenant Jaques who led a patrol was killed.

Air Cavalry Goes to Khe Sanh

President Johnson and his advisors were terrified for weeks of a full-scale assault on Khe Sanh, similar to General Giap's 1954 Viet Minh victory over the French base at Dien Bien Phu. General Tolson, Commander of the 1st Cavalry Division (Airmobile), devised a plan for the relief of Khe Sanh. In late March we got the word

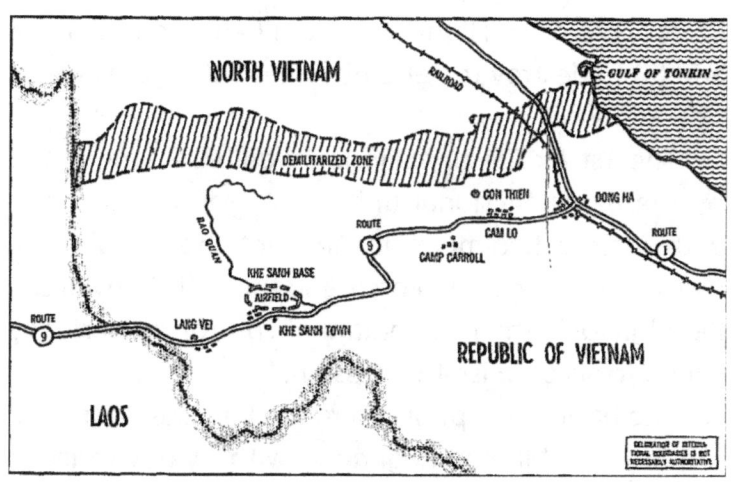

Marines at Khe Sanh.

we were going to Khe Sanh. Operation Pegasus' mission was threefold: (1) to relieve the Khe Sanh Combat Base; (2) to open Highway 9 from Cà Lu to Khe Sanh; and (3) to destroy the enemy forces within the area of operations.

The 1st Air Cavalry Division would be augmented by these nondivisional units—1st Marine Regiment, 26th Marine Regiment, III Army of the Republic of Vietnam Airborne Task Force, and the 37th Army of the Republic of Vietnam operational control, all perfectly suited to accomplish the mission.

The basic concept of Operation Pegasus was:

The 1st Marine Regiment with two battalions

would launch a ground attack west toward Khe Sanh while the 1st Cavalry 3rd Brigade would lead the air assault. On D+1 and D+2 all elements would continue to attack west toward Khe Sanh; and, on the following day, the 2nd Brigade of the Cavalry would land three battalions southeast of Khe Sanh and attack northwest. The 26th Marine Regiment, which was holding Khe Sanh, would attack south to secure Hill 471. On D+4, the 1st Brigade would air assault just south of Khe Sanh and attack north. The following day the 3rd Army of the Republic of Vietnam Airborne Task Force would air assault southwest of Khe Sanh and attack toward Lang Vei Special Forces Camp. Linkup was planned at the end of seven days.

Operation Pegasus—Relief of Khe Sanh

April 1, 1968, 2/7 Cav (my battalion, part of 3rd Brigade) went by chopper to LZ Cà Lu (Stud) which was the main staging area for Operation Pegasus. From there we were to go to LZ Thor—a location to be determined later.

We air assaulted to the top of a mountain. The terrain was thick jungle, grassy, and mountainous. I saw bomb strikes in the distance at night—"Arc Lights"—B-52 carpet bombing of NVA troops and materiel as the sky lit

Operation Pegasus: Landing Zone Cà Lu (Stud).

up and the ground shook. The Air Force was prepping the area before we conducted our combat air assaults. It was exciting and scary.

April 2 was a sunny day. We were on a high mountaintop surrounded by a river on three sides. The weather was nice, and I was comfortable sleeping in my poncho liner the night before. D Company (mine) got a log (logistic) ship (helicopter) with food and water. The old Army expression, "Hurry up and wait," is so perfectly accurate. We just waited to go on the next mission, and choppers eventually came to pick us up. My platoon was in the lead.

Vietnam Anti-War Movement—the Great American Con Job

Air Cavalry on an air assult to their objective during Operation Pegasus, 1968.

We (D Company) led the air assault heading toward Khe Sanh. When we were in the air prior to dismounting the helicopters, I saw a downed jet in a ravine below. I thought that if the NVA could shoot down jets they certainly could shoot down helicopters. The metal "skin" on a Huey helicopter is very thin. Even though we might be flying into eternity, I loved to ride in the helicopter. We approached the LZ (landing zone), "dismounted" the helicopters, and took cover in gigantic bomb craters left by massive B-52 bombing. The rich, soft upturned dirt from the bomb explosions made gigantic craters and great predug foxholes. No shots were fired.

When we exited the choppers, I assembled my platoon in a modified column formation to recon the area. We were "on point" for the battalion.

We did not carry our "butt packs," but we had web gear, C-rations, fragmentation and smoke grenades, M-16 ammunition, ammo belts for M-60s, LAWs (light antitank weapons), PRC-25s (radios), and a 90 mm recoilless rifle. My M-79 grenadiers previously traded in their M-79s for 12-gauge pump shotguns with buckshot or flechette shotgun shells because the jungle was

Soldier carrying a recoilless rifle.

very thick. Some wore flak vests, but we avoided doing so whenever we could. My point man that day was a guy we called "Hippy." He was a lanky guy and had a peace symbol on his helmet, and he was an excellent point man—the first guy in order of movement as we moved cautiously through "Indian country." Hippy found a machine gun site and an NVA helmet and a bag of raw opium. The NVA used opium for medicinal purposes and perhaps to prepare themselves for sapper (suicide) attacks. I told Hippy to take the bag back to turn it in. I don't know if he ever did. It was worth a lot of money. He may still be living off of it.

April 3, our company moved through dense, thick vegetation in a company column formation like a large snake winding through it. The 3rd Platoon was point platoon on this advance. As the company moved through the jungle, we were strung out over a long distance.

We knew that 3rd platoon up ahead was in contact with the NVA because the semi- and fully automatic weapons fire and explosions announced the firefight throughout the jungle. In a firefight, you did not see a person shooting at you—bushes shot at you. The NVA had a special knack of dragging away their casualties immediately so that, although you knew you hit someone, as soon as you got to their location, they were gone. It was ominous. It was as though the NVA were ghosts. In my view, "body count" was a false sense of success on the battlefield.

A popular young NCO in 3rd Platoon was killed in action this day. He went to retrieve an enemy RPD (light machine gun) and was killed. The S-3 (operations officer) brought him back and placed him on the ground near my position in front of me.

Before he set down the dead soldier on the ground, the body started regurgitating—the involuntary action of the body after death. I had never seen that before. There is nothing as permanent as death.

I often had bouts with internal terror, but I could not show fear as I was leading about 40 men and trying to keep them alive, while at the same time accomplishing whatever mission we were given. The NVA were great fighters who fought the Japanese, later the French, and then the Americans. But we won all the major combat actions, and we were able to control the area we chose to control.

Later in the afternoon, we moved to this Hill-242 near Route 9 and set up a company-size perimeter. We were in a combination of jungle and forest and had to clear trees for a Landing Zone (LZ) to get resupplies from helicopters. We wrapped "det cord" (detonation cord filled with explosives, which burns at thousands of feet per second) around smaller trees and blew them in two, but there were too many trees, and we were unsuccessful in this task.

One of the other units took a mule (small flatbed utility vehicle) and tried to bring us supplies along the road. They were ambushed—some were KIA. They should not have assumed that the road was secure because NVA were all around. We didn't get food or water all day; so, we gathered rainwater on our ponchos tied to trees to catch it. We made fortifications and overhead cover. We got mortared that day, and 10 or 11 of my men got minor wounds from mortar shrapnel and were extracted from our perimeter by a jungle penetrator—like a heavy plumb bob dropped through jungle canopy so a person can sit on and be lifted to the helicopter.

They all survived and returned to my platoon. Medivac helicopters were a great contribution to modern warfare. None of my men were killed while under my command because we were incredibly lucky and because we were rather good soldiers.

My platoon sergeant and I were checking the perimeter looking at the surrounding thick jungle vegetation. Visibility was only a few feet. Suddenly, we heard from outside our perimeter that distinctive clank of the bolt of an AK-47 being pulled back. I yelled, "Get down," and we pancaked to the ground as the automatic weapons fire started chopping the leaves above, and they fell on us.

When that AK opened-up, one of our young black troopers pumped his M-60 fire into the direction of the enemy fire. That M-60 just kept spewing automatic weapon's fire and never jammed once. He probably saved my life. I got him that new M-60 machine gun prior to heading to Khe Sanh. Just another time I was almost killed.

An interesting situation occurred that night. Two of my RTOs (radio men) were near me at our makeshift fortification, so I had constant commo. That night I heard the company commander on the radio state that it appeared there were NVA artillery rounds that landed in our perimeter but did not explode. He said that they could be "duds" or chemical agents. I stayed awake all night thinking I'd die from a nerve agent. I was glad to see the sun come up.

April 4, we moved back to a position where the 105 mm howitzers had been brought in by Chinook helicopters to get supplies.

As we came back, we picked up a couple of the dead and wounded who tried yesterday to get us supplies

Vietnam Anti-War Movement—the Great American Con Job

Chinook helicopter, Vietnam.

by going down the road on the mule. We manned the company perimeter and saw more dead and wounded who had been recovered.

The second platoon leader of C Company was killed, and I identified with him and his death since I was second platoon leader of D Company. Seeing his body (shot four times) really bothered me. One Medevac chopper was shot up. The NVA were dangerous, and I didn't like this area and hoped we all would get out alive.

We didn't have any food or water the day before and for most of this day, and everyone was exhausted.

After a while, I got almost numb to the idea that I was mortal and could be killed at any time. I had been scared before but always did my best to hide it as I was the platoon "leader."

In my view, if anyone has ever been in real combat and said he was never scared—he's simply a liar. My mind could keep me somewhat detached when I saw the dead and wounded; but when I saw the 2nd platoon leader of C Company dead, I really personalized this.

April 5, I got the word that our battalion would make the walk to Khe Sanh the next day. Based on everything I heard about Khe Sanh and what I had seen, I thought this could be disastrous. The Marines had been continuously shelled and surrounded by superior forces and were holding on to control the area for the previously stated reasons. We were aware of the news reports which made Khe Sanh sound like "hell."

We had incurred a lot of dead and wounded since we had been there, and I had a lot of close calls. Everyone feared the area.

The NVA were numerous and good fighters. We dug in again for the night as jets kept circling the hill we occupied. A lot of choppers were in the air, and artillery kept pounding the surrounding areas.

April 6, we tried to walk from this LZ to Khe Sanh, but we had to come back as the two forward companies received effective fire. Our company was supposed to air assault to 500 meters east of Khe Sanh combat base. I thought that this was a glory "push" to see who could be the first to walk into Khe Sanh. I hoped we would make it because we had a lot of reporters with us.

Later on, General John J. Tolson, the 1st Cavalry's Division commander, wrote in *Vietnam Studies– Airmobility 1961-1971*: that:

> *"...the heaviest contact on April 6 occurred in the 3d Brigade's area of operation as the 2d Battalion, 7th Cavalry, continued its drive west on Highway Nine. In a daylong battle which ended when the enemy summarily abandoned his position and fled, the battalion had 83 NVA killed, one POW captured, and 121 individual and ten crew-served weapons captured."*

Tolson further wrote that:

> *"... the 1st Cavalry Division troops were airlifted to Hill 471, relieving the Marines at this position. This was the first relief of the defenders of*

Khe Sanh. Two companies of troopers remained on the hill while two other companies attacked to the south toward the Khe Sanh hamlet. The 1st Cavalry forces on landing zone Snapper were attacked by an enemy force using mortars, hand grenades, and rocket launchers.

The attack was a disaster for the enemy, and twenty were killed. The 84th Company of the Vietnamese 8th Airborne Battalion was airlifted by 1st Cavalry Division aircraft into Khe Sanh Combat Base and linked up with elements of the 37th Ranger Battalion. The lift was conducted without incident and was the official link-up of forces at Khe Sanh."

Although 1st Cavalry units relieved Marines at Hill 471 and airlifted Vietnamese Airborne into KSCB (Khe Sanh Combat Base), Route 9 still had to be cleared to the base. It was common practice for commanders to rotate personnel or units as point elements for various reasons—to share the risk of being "point," to allow recuperation of a unit, or to use the best people or unit to accomplish the mission. On this day, it was other units' (companies and platoons in the battalion) turn to be the "point" in order of movement. We were last in order of movement, and we thought we got a break.

As we moved through the jungle, I heard a firefight up ahead (automatic weapons fire and explosions) as the forward companies "made contact" with the NVA, and we were ordered to reverse direction of movement and go back to the road to be picked up by chopper and leapfrog over those companies and continue the mission to clear Route 9. My platoon was on point again.

April 7, we air assaulted near the top of a mountain that seemed to be solid rock. As my platoon approached the crest, I heard bullets whistle overhead and noticed that the ground had no cover and was just

2/7 Cavalry troopers on their way to Khe Sanh

too hard to dig in if we had to. We just kept moving toward the crest.

My point squad radioed that they saw bunkers as they approached, so I had the platoon get in an "on line" formation so all firepower would be to the front.

We were in the open with no cover. I expected a firefight any second, so we cautiously continued the advance. My M-16 selector switch was on "fire"—not "safe." We came to the crest of the hill and found NVA fighting positions in a regimental-size NVA complex of bunkers, tunnels, and all kinds of weapons—mortars, machine guns, antiaircraft guns. (See photos.)

The NVA made their defensive perimeter right on Route 9. We found ZPU-4s (anticraft guns), AKs, RPDs, RPKs (light machine guns), RPGs (rocket propelled grenade launchers and ammo), commo wire linking bunkers, and dead NVA soldiers in bunkers with blood coming out of their ears, probably due to the constant air force bombing in the area. The NVA had run commo wire between their bunkers for constant communication.

One of my guys, nicknamed "Turtle," found an old French bugle and made a tassel for it out of parachute cord. He said he found the bugle in a trench, and while putting the cord on it, a cobra snake rose up, puffed

Vietnam Anti-War Movement—the Great American Con Job

NVA mortar rounds and weapons found at NVA base camp.

NVA Bugle captured near Khe Sanh

out, and he shot it with a .38 snub-nosed pistol he carried. It was his personal weapon and was unauthorized, but it came in handy that day. Turtle brought the cobra stuck on an SKS rifle bayonet to show us. It was a beautiful bluish- and silver-colored creature, pretty much shot up. Turtle must have put all six rounds into the snake. He gave me the bugle. I got an AK-47, an NVA bayonet, and an ammo pouch as souvenirs. I have all the items except the AK.

The area was pockmarked with bomb craters courtesy of the U.S. Air Force. The bombing was probably the result of Arc Lights. The jet jocks can brag about how sexy their "fighters" are, but I love B-52s, and I especially love Hueys.

We were about two miles outside of Khe Sanh, and

this NVA bunker complex was abandoned, but Route 9 to Khe Sanh still had to be cleared.

Only Two Miles to Khe Sanh

My platoon was tasked to lead the clearing action. We were the point platoon for the battalion, brigade, and division. We had to avoid the "toe poppers" (explosive bomblets dropped by the Air Force) and other potential booby traps as we cautiously proceeded along Route 9, and we still did not know the status of the NVA as we moved along.

As we moved down the road, I had some of my men straddle the road by 30 to 40 meters to be flank security. I kept my RTOs nearby for commo with whomever I needed to have contact with, especially my squads—each squad had its own radio. Our weapons were "at the ready" as we did not know what awaited us, and I knew that we could be ambushed at any moment because the Marines from Khe Sanh Combat Base could not move up and down Route 9 for over two months. Some say that all the NVA left the area, but all they had to do was slip over the Laotian border and cross back and forth. I think that is what they did.

When Lang Vei Special Forces camp was attacked in

February by NVA with tanks, the Marine contingency to go down Route 9 as a relief force for Lang Vei could not be implemented because the NVA controlled the area. This was the same road we were on now. The area was deadly. There were bunkers strategically placed along the road all the way to the wire at Khe Sanh to ambush anyone going down the road. We found NVA backpacks, opium, weapons, etc.—but the NVA had vanished.

My platoon led the movement for two miles to the Marine base, and we were ordered to stay outside the wire. I made a personal diary entry:

"Sunday, April 7, 1700 hrs. We are at Khe Sanh camped outside the east entrance on Highway 9."

On April 8, my platoon was the first platoon to walk into Khe Sanh. We were the tip of the spear of the 1st Air Cavalry Division relief force as we entered the wire perimeter at Khe Sanh, single file. We were *on point*. I led the column of Air Cavalry troopers as we crossed past the concertina wire.

As we entered the Khe Sanh perimeter wire, we were in a file formation. My company commander asked me if I could play that NVA bugle. In junior high and first two years of high school, I played trumpet, so

Vietnam Anti-War Movement—the Great American Con Job

Above: 1st Cav troops entering Khe Sanh. Below: U.S. Marines stand by the road leading through Khe Sanh as members of Company "B", 5th Battalion, 7th Cavalry, 3rd Brigade, pass on their way to Hill 680, April 1968.

as I entered the perimeter wire at the head of the division column, I played the cavalry charge bugle call on the NVA bugle. We probably were a sight as 1st Cavalry troopers walked into Khe Sanh—I had my M-16 and AK-47 and was blowing "charge" on an NVA bugle. My lips were dry, and I hadn't played a trumpet in years, but it sounded like the "cavalry charge."

We all knew this was a big deal at the time because Khe Sanh was all over the press. The Marines held the "fort" until we got there and ended the siege.

A Marine captain told me where to place my platoon to provide security along the air strip. My platoon of about 40 men covered the side of the air strip normally manned by 150-200 Marines. I put about four men per bunker in bunkers about 30 meters apart along the air strip. We really needed more men to do the job right.

I stayed awake all night, scared to death, expecting a bonsai charge. I saw "Spooky" or "Puff" (heavily armed C-130 aircraft) fire tracer rounds into what appeared to be Laos. No bonsai charge occurred.

I made another diary entry:

"Today, D Company was the first to walk into Khe Sanh on Highway 9 in two months. The

Marines have been pinned in but now they can move. My platoon was the first in. This place is bunkers and trenches. The incoming artillery is deadly... Everything is in bunkers beneath the ground as the NVA continually shoot artillery here. My company—D, 2nd of the 7th Cav—was the first unit to walk into Khe Sanh. My platoon walked in first. Newsmen, etc., were all around as we probably did something significant .... This could be a turning point in the war. I hope all goes well. Anyway, we walked in on Highway 9, where no one before could travel because of ambushes. We cleared it..."

The siege was officially over, and it was the 1st Cavalry that ended it. I realize that some Marines don't like the idea that the Cavalry came to their rescue (in fact, they deny it). I guess it's a *macho* thing, but it is what it is, or, it was what it was. Marines who were there at Khe Sanh at the time will tell the truth. Several have told me they remember seeing the 1st Cav coming in and were glad to see us.

Joe Abodeely

*Above: Nardi and Lutz with Khe Sanh sign.
Below: 2nd platoon D/2/7 Cavalry, 1st Cavalry Division (Airmobile).
I am front left, kneeling with the sunglasses.*

Vietnam Anti-War Movement—the Great American Con Job

The *Los Angeles Herald Examiner* on April 8 reported:

"A two-mile victorious march by the Army 1st Air Cavalry Division formally ended the 78-day Communist siege of the fort Hanoi vowed it would take and American generals pledged would never be lost. The siege was over but the battle for control of South Vietnam's Communist-infested northern frontier roared on...

At Khe Sanh, where round-the-clock Communist artillery fire had driven 6000 Marine defenders underground, the Leathernecks Sunday whooped it up as Army 1st Lt. Joe Abodeely's unit walked the last two miles into the camp. Abodeely, 24, of Tucson, Ariz., and his platoon formed the 1st Air Cavalry spearhead of the 20,000-man Operation Pegasus drive that broke the Communist grip around Khe Sanh in a weeklong drive that covered 12 miles of jungle, hills, and minefields..."

General Tolson wrote in *Vietnam Studies–Airmobility 1961-1971*:

"...it became increasingly evident, through lack of contact and the large amounts of new equipment being found indiscriminately abandoned on the battlefield, that the enemy had fled the area rather than face certain defeat. He was totally confused by the swift, bold, many-pronged attacks... April 8, at 0800, the relief of Khe Sanh was affected, and the 1st Cavalry Division became the new landlord."

The 1st Air Cavalry Division's mobility, maneuverability, and fire power minimized U.S. causalities and ended the 77-day long siege of Khe Sanh.

Media and the War

At the beginning of the Vietnam War, the press had little interest. The few reports focused on the rise of Communism in-country, but since the beginning of World War II, television gradually became familiar to the public, and by the war's end, television was manufactured in large scale.

In the 1950s, only 9% of American homes had a television. During 1960 and 1964, the war came to many American living rooms and usually with bad news. Without adequate government controls, the media published uncensored photos and videos showing the brutality of the Vietnam War, vastly influencing public opinion in unprecedented proportions.

New recording technologies like the video camera and audio recorder helped journalists and reporters capture many more photographs and recorded video materials. As a result, the government faced a huge challenge in censoring all news media—a task they had done in World War I and World War II by using strict policy.

By the end of 1960, the death of many civilians in a coup against President Diem started to change the views on Vietnam. The public did not know that Communists had infiltrated Buddhist factions and instigated conflicts between ARVN troops and Communist sympathizers. Soon after that, the *New York Times* sent their first reporter to Saigon, followed by Reuters, Agency France Press, Times, etc.

In a survey conducted in 1964, 58% of U.S. residents said they "got most of their news" from television. In 1966, it was 93%. Television was the most important source of news for the American people during the Vietnam War era.

In 1964, the media described the battle of Ap Bac as a debacle of the South Vietnamese Army. The Buddhist crisis highlighted by the famous photo of the monk's self-immolation portrayed Diem's regime as brutal and dictatorial.

The Vietnam War is often referred to as the "first television war" as film from Vietnam was flown to Tokyo for quick developing and editing and then flown on to the U.S. The important stories could be transmitted directly by satellite from Tokyo. Most television stories were filmed soon after a battle rather than in the midst of one.

Many were simply conventional news stories. Most stories about the war on nightly TV news shows were not film records fresh from Vietnam, but rather brief reports based on wire service dispatches and read by anchormen. Unfortunately, the real time killing and destruction, filmed and presented to the U.S. public, was sufficiently dramatic to alienate the public from the war.

The media began to influence public opinion in a negative way, and that became a matter of concern to the U.S. government. In order to deal with a large number of press corps, the U.S. had to develop a more effective method to control the correspondents.

The U.S. Mission and Military Assistance Command, Vietnam (MACV) appointed an "information czar," Barry Zorthian, to advise General Westmoreland about information policy. As the war became more intense, the press corps in South Vietnam increased rapidly. From just 40 in 1964, the number jumped to 419 in August 1965.

From 1965 to 1967, Barry Zorthian, experienced in the media, got things done well. In almost all the nightly news programs of major television networks like CBS and NBC, the war was presented as "good guys shooting Reds" story. The media generally supported U.S. involvement in Vietnam. By 1968, at the height of the war, there were about 600 accredited journalists of all nationalities in Vietnam, reporting for U.S. wire services, radio and television networks, and the major newspaper chains and news magazines.

The U.S. Military Assistance Command, Vietnam (MACV) made military transportation readily available to news people, and some took advantage of this frequently to venture into the field and get their stories firsthand. That proximity to the battlefield carried obvious risks, and more than 60 journalists were killed during the war.

Many reporters, however, spent most of their time in the South Vietnamese capitol, Saigon (now Ho Chi Minh City), and got their stories from the Joint U.S. Public Affairs Office's daily briefings (which soon became known as "the five o'clock follies").

The role of the media in the Vietnam War is a subject of continuing controversy. Some believe that the media played a large role in the conclusion of the Vietnam War and that the media's tendency toward negative reporting helped to undermine support for the war in the United States while its uncensored coverage provided valuable information to the enemy in Vietnam.

Vietnam Anti-War Movement—the Great American Con Job

Although media reporting prior to 1968 may have been supportive of the U.S. effort then, the subsequent false reporting about Tet 1968 and the U.S. effort through the Paris Peace Accords, and even up to present time, has been negative and deceptive. The scenes of bloody fighting in Hue, Saigon, and other cities in Vietnam during Tet really shocked the American people who experienced war for the first time on their television sets.

The Tet Offensive at the end of January 1968, changed the media's coverage of the war. Although the offensive was clearly a military victory for South Vietnam, the U.S. media spun it as a victory for the Communists by focusing on a few difficult combat actions like the Battle of Hue or the Viet Cong attack on the U.S. Embassy or the siege of Marines at Khe Sanh.

After Tet, media coverage of the war showing images of civilian and military casualties were increasingly televised. The pressure to withdraw from the war became overwhelming after Tet.

Television daily fed the controversy to malign the war. On February 14, 1968, Walter Cronkite prepared a report—never shown to the public—that the Tet attacks were a failure.

But on the February 1967, assessment by Walter

Walter Cronkite

Cronkite, the anchor of the CBS Evening News, was that the conflict was "mired in stalemate." Cronkite revised his report and said: *"…the only rational way out then will be to negotiate, not as victors, but as an honorable people who lived up to their pledge to defend democracy and did the best, they could…"*

The "most trusted man in America" and other members of the media did not report that the U.S. military and the ARVN (Army of the Republic of Vietnam) won all the major battles of the Tet Offensive, and there was little reporting about the Communist atrocities.

He misled the public. This was misrepresentation

by omission. Other newscasters misrepresented the conduct of the war and further incited the various anti-war factions. It was a perfect storm to disparage U.S. military involvement. Cronkite's report on Tet was seen by many as the signal of a sea change in reporting about Vietnam.

The percentage of "victory stories" decreased to 44 from 62 after Tet. Many iconic photos of the war, such as the execution of the Viet Cong guerilla by the ARVN colonel, or the napalm hit on the village (actually done by the Vietnamese Air Force) with the naked little girl running away, exerted a negative and lasting influence on the public feeling. As the war was portrayed uglier on screen, public support declined significantly.

Media power was noted by President Johnson who said, "If I've lost Cronkite, I've lost Middle America." American disillusionment with the war stemmed from many causes, of which the media was only one.

The scenes of bloody fighting in Hue, Saigon, and other cities in Vietnam during Tet really shocked the American people who experienced the war on their television sets. America needed a "win" that the media would report—*maybe something like the cavalry riding to the rescue of a besieged fort as portrayed in an old Western movie.*

Some say that what most weakened support for the war was simply the level of American casualties: the greater the increase in casualties, the lower the level of public support for the war. But casualties from the invasion of Normandy exceeded all the American deaths in Vietnam, and the American public did not see it on television.

During World War II, the U.S. press presented what the government allowed. The death reports for Vietnam rose in 1968 and 1969. Anti-war protests raged in the continental U.S., and the public mood turned hostile. It was not the number of deaths; it was public awareness of the number of deaths in the nightly television news reports that disheartened the American public.

Historians and the War

The Vietnam War still has a negative image for many. Its veterans and the war are often depicted unfavorably or simply ignored, but attitudes change with education about the truth of the war. The Vietnam War is barely studied or discussed amenably in high school or college although its study is still relevant and of interest and matters to those who served.

A serious problem studying the Vietnam War is the blind acceptance of dubious writings from the triumvirate of Halberstam, Sheehan, and Karnow, journalists, not historians, reporting on the war as it was happening and later writing best-selling books. In the fall of 1963, they publicly vilified President Diem's regime claiming Vietnam would be better off without him. They portrayed Diem's regime as illegitimate and "tyrannical" and his discrimination against the Buddhists as oppressive.

Halberstam printed adverse material before the

other journalists—*The Making of a Quagmire* in 1964, *Ho*, in 1971, and *The Best and the Brightest*, in 1972. Karnow published *Vietnam: A History*, a multivolume PBS documentary in 1983, selling over one million copies. Sheehan's *A Bright Shining Lie*, in 1988, won the national book award and Pulitzer Prize.

These journalists thought Diem was not liberal enough in dealing with the press and the Buddhist protesters. They didn't believe Diem's claim that the Communists infiltrated the Buddhists, which the Communists later admitted that they did. In November 1963, the Buddhist generals got JFK's approval to kill Diem and his brother in a coup three weeks before JFK's assassination.

A small group of veterans and academic historians rejected the basic tenets of the anti-war movement and produced works called *revisionist*. Some "orthodox" scholars believed the revisionists' primary goal was to distort facts about the Vietnam War to justify U.S. involvement in the war.

Revisionists made progress in the late 1990s with histories arguing that South Vietnam grew much stronger by the early 1970s and had, during this period, with the help of the United States, wiped out the Viet Cong insurgents. U.S. forces left Vietnam in 1973, and

Saigon was taken over in 1975—two years later—after Congress reneged on its promise to fund South Vietnam's military.

What would have happened if the U.S. honored its word to fund South Vietnam after the U.S. left? I think they could have kept their country and there would not have been any "boat people." Revisionist numbers eventually increased, but the movement never made major inroads into academia.

Dr. Mark Moyar, Director, USAID Office of Civilian-Military Cooperation, authored several books and worked extensively on national security affairs, international development, foreign aid, and capacity building. His article, "Vietnam: Historians at War," about journalists misrepresenting the Vietnam War, is elucidating. The following are other examples of "revisionists."

Marguerite Higgins, the first female war correspondent to win the Pulitzer Prize reporting on the Korean War, saw that Halberstam's articles had clear inaccuracies to tarnish President Diem. She authored *New York Herald Tribune* stories gutting many of his claims.

The Times editor sent Halberstam a letter stating that Higgins' writing balanced his negative material from Saigon, and he wanted Halberstam to cover that aspect of the RVN story. This infuriated and embarrassed Halberstam who threatened to quit if they published Higgins' articles.

Higgins wrote a book in 1965 entitled *Our Vietnam Nightmare*. It was not as popular as the books by Halberstam, Sheehan, and Karnow. In a few years it faded into obscurity.

A small group of revisionist books emerged in the 1970s and 1980s. Many of their authors had doctorates, but few had permanent academic appointments.

Robert F. Turner, Vietnam veteran, Hoover Institution Fellow, worked in Britain in a history department less politicized than in the U.S. He later got a nontenured position at the University of Virginia Law School and disputed that the Vietnamese Communists were devoted nationalists in his book *Vietnamese Communism: Its Origins and Development*.

Other "revisionist" writers were Ralph Smith, distinguished British professor, who, in an international history of the war, argued that Vietnamese communism was a serious threat to the U.S.; Norman Podhoretz, the American pundit, made the same argument in a work geared more for the public than academia; and Ellen Hammer and William Colby, an American scholar living in France and a former CIA director, respectively, alleged South Vietnam was viable under Diem and the U.S. seriously erred in inspiring his demise.

Veterans like Harry Summers and former President Nixon argued the war could have been won had the U.S. taken more aggressive military actions to sever the Ho Chi Minh trail in Laos and increase massive bombing in North Vietnam. History has shown that they were right.

Guenter Lewy's *America in Vietnam*, the most influential of the early revisionist books, was the refutation of anti-war arguments about the immorality, inhumanity, and illegality of U.S. military actions in Vietnam. After Lewy's book, countless trendy anti-war arguments stopped appearing in the articles and books written by the anti-war authors.

Arthur Dommen's *The Indochinese Experience of the French and the Americans: Nationalism and Communism in Cambodia, Laos, and Vietnam* is the longest work of recent revisionism. He was a journalist in South Vietnam and Laos during the war and later obtained a Ph.D. in agricultural economics; and he spent many years gathering information, including from the Vietnamese.

He debunked the Halberstam-Sheehan-Karnow

accounts and stressed the evils of Vietnamese Communism, and he concluded Diem, a nationalist, and his supporters, was a viable leader. He was one of the first to say that Buddhist protesters made up evidence of religious oppression to cripple South Vietnam's government from 1963 to 1965 and were more concerned with gaining political power than religious freedom.

Lewis Sorley, a veteran of the U.S. Army and CIA who also has a Ph.D., but no academic affiliation, wrote about regular and irregular elements of the war during its latter years in his book *A Better War*. He supported revisionists' views that South Vietnam was feasible and could have survived if the U.S. had not cut aid to it in the final years of the war.

Sorley showed that as American forces gradually withdrew, South Vietnam forces improved greatly and were able to defeat a massive offensive by fourteen North Vietnamese divisions in the spring of 1972—an event orthodox historians ignored.

B.G. Burkett, a Vietnam veteran and a stockbroker by profession, demolished most of the mythology surrounding Vietnam veterans in his book *Stolen Valor*, extraordinary for its detailed research and its nationwide popularity. His book showed that several hundred made-up Vietnam veterans in the public spotlight were frauds.

Burkett used statistics and detective work to disprove orthodox historians' long-held generalizations that Vietnam veterans had much higher rates of unemployment, homelessness, and suicide than nonveterans.

For decades since the war, there has been this schizophrenic attempt by Vietnam-era persons to either claim they were in Vietnam when they were not or to deny they were in Vietnam when they were. Some of the imposters are detected when they make VA claims or are "outed" when joining a veteran's organization.

Some don't want the stigma of Vietnam service while others don't want the stigma of not having Vietnam service. Others claim Vietnam veteran service for VA benefits—medical examinations, treatment, medicine, loans, burial, perceived heroic image, etc.

Epilogue

The Vietnam War was not just a war—it was an experience for those who served in it and for their family and friends. The war was also an experience for those who had political agendas and used the war as a means to promote those causes.

There has been much written about the Vietnam War, with differing perspectives regarding its causes, conduct, and results; therefore, it is difficult to gauge what the majority of people think about the war today. Warriors throughout history have been respected and honored for their service to the clan, tribe, or nation, but NOT Vietnam War warriors. Why did this happen? Maybe it was because Vietnam veterans lacked the power or know-how to defend their service since they were busy defending their country's interests and getting on with their lives.

Vietnam is a complex subject worthy of study and discussion. If you played a word game in which you were

Vietnam Anti-War Movement—the Great American Con Job

asked to associate just one word with "Vietnam," what would it be? Patriotism? Communism? War? Debacle? Cause? Betrayal? Loss? Shame? Duty? History? Or is it two words—"Who cares?" One-tenth of military age males then served in the war; and those who are still alive, and their families, care.

To many, the Vietnam War is ancient history and is often misrepresented, but we owe to it those who served in it and are still alive, to tell the truth about their service. Many Vietnam veterans have a bond irrespective of their backgrounds and life's experiences, and they understand each other when others do not.

Everyone who served in Vietnam has a perspective, and over 90% are proud of their service. My perspective is not the first nor will it be the last, but I hope it may contribute to a better understanding of the U.S. servicemen's role in Vietnam.

Much anti-war history and information was inaccurate or biased in favor of the "anti-war movement," including opportunists in media, academia, and government. Still others were disgruntled veterans, politicians, clergy, draft dodgers, and groups such as blacks, women, Mexicans, gays, "liberals," and Communist sympathizers.

The Vietnam War was a noble cause. The U.S. went

to war under the authority of an international treaty to protect the people of South Vietnam from Communist expansion. U.S. troops should have been welcomed home and not been denied jobs or not been greeted with jeers, riots, and anti-war protests. They should not be forgotten. The best way to truly honor Vietnam veterans is to tell the truth about their war and their successes, such as winning battles; achieving medical, technological, and military advancements; and saving South Vietnam before they left Vietnam.

Vietnam soldiers served about 240 days on the average in combat, while World War II veterans served maybe 40 days in combat. Two-thirds of Vietnam veterans volunteered while only one-third volunteered in World War II. They were the most educated who served, and they fought well. Over 90% of Vietnam veterans are justifiably proud of their service since they won all the battles, the Tet Offensive, and ended the war, achieving a peace treaty in 1973. They deserved to be respected.

The bravery of the Marines holding out at Khe Sanh and the mobility, firepower, and successes of Air Cavalry units have been lost to history. The many battles—Gulf of Tonkin Incident, Pleiku, Qui Nhon, Van Tuong, Ia Drang, Tet Offensive 1968, Hue, Khe Sanh,

Firebase Ripcord, Easter Offensive, Xuan Loc, *Mayaguez* incident, and other actions, known and unknown—all had their heroes.

The public attitude toward Vietnam veterans has changed since many organizations and veterans have discovered how to capitalize on catering to veterans' needs, real and fraudulent. Politicians used to use a phrase, *"Let's do it for the children."* Now, it's, *"Let's do it for the veterans,"* and some "veterans" may milk the public good will.

The present-day image of veterans has morphed from "heroes" to "victims," and the more "victim" one can appear to be, the more public benefits he can receive—while other veterans are maligned. There have been phony "heroes" or imposters who stole veterans' honor by claiming Vietnam service, military awards, or deeds when they never served in Vietnam. We should expose and challenge imposters who criticize U.S. service in Vietnam.

Historians, journalists, and politicians should tell the truth if we expect future generations to risk their lives in the service of our country, and educational institutions should correct the slanted history of the Vietnam War. Hopefully, someday, our country will correct the record before these veterans get any older and newer issues grab the public's interest. Maybe it's already too late. We need to treat veterans of the Vietnam War as the heroes they are, not as victims, and let them know we value their service. And mean it!

Colonel Joe Abodeely, USA (Ret) 8-23-2020

About the Author

Joe Abodeely was born in Tucson, Arizona in 1943. His education from grade school to Law School was in Tucson. A war was brewing, and he went to Vietnam in January 1968 as an Infantry Lieutenant. Assigned to the 1st Cavalry Division (Airmobile) AKA "the 1st Air Cavalry" (think Apocalypse Now or We Were Soldiers), he saw action during the bloodiest year of the war in the unit that saw the most combat. Upon returning home after his one-year tour, he was astonished and chagrined to see firsthand the public's disrespect for those risking their lives for their country.

Joe has practiced law for nearly 50 years, founded the Arizona Military Museum serving as its chief executive officer for over 40 years, presented annual dinners commemorating Vietnam veterans' service, and has been an outspoken advocate for those who honorably served in the Vietnam War. He is author of Dear Mom and Dad, Love From Vietnam (recipient of three Global E-book Awards). This is his second book.

Recommended Reading

Abodeely, Joe. *Dear Mom and Dad, Love from Vietnam*, Desert Bugle Press (2014).

Brown, William F. *Our Vietnam Wars*, Volume 3. (2019).

Hammel, Eric. *The Siege of Khe Sanh: An Oral History*, Warner Books (1989).

Lewis, John E. *The Mammoth Book of War Diaries and Letters*, editor, Carroll and Graf (1999).

Edited by Morgan, Speer and Michalson, Greg. *For Our Beloved Country*, Atlantic Monthly Press (1994).

Mark Moyar, *Historians at War*, U.S. Marine Corps University, Quantico (Spring 2008).

Prados, John and Stubbe, Ray. *Valley of Decision: The Siege of Khe Sanh*, Dell Publishing (1991).

Shaw, Geoffrey. *The Lost Mandate of Heaven, The American Betrayal of Ngo Dinh Diem, President of Vietnam*, Ignatius Press (2015).

Stanton, Shelby L. *The 1st Cav in Vietnam, Anatomy of a Division*, Ballantine Books (1987).

Tolson, Lieutenant General John J. *Vietnam Studies—Airmobility 1961-1971*, Department of the Army, Washington (1999).

Credits

COVER CREDITS:

Front cover:
Breedlove, Howard C. "**Operation "Oregon"**, a search and destroy mission conducted by an infantry platoon of Troop B, First Reconnaissance Squadron, 9th Calvary, First Calvary Division (Airmobile), three kilometers west of Duc Pho, Quang Ngai Province, Vietnam on April 24, 1967. Members of the reconnaissance platoon are dispatched from an UH-1D helicopter hovering above the ridge line. U.S. Army. Almay.com. ID: EG707A. Used with permission.

Harold Adler. "**Vietnam protesters, close up.**" Alamy.com. ID: P1W1TR. Used with permission.

__. "**Anti-war demonstrators outside an army induction center in NYC chant, 'Hell no, we won't go'.**" December 6, 1967. CSU Archives / Everett Collection. Used with permission.

Vejcik, Marian. "Flag." iStockphoto. used with permission.

Back cover:
Baxter, Allen. "**American Flags.**" iStockphoto. Used with permission.

Joe Abodeely

"List of Protests" from Wikipedia on page 34:
Wikipedia contributors, Wikipedia.com. Accessed on 8/25/20 https://en.wikipedia. org/w/index.php?title=List_of_protests_against_the_Vietnam_War&oldid=973365665.

p. vi. __. "**Minority group from University of Pennsylvania seem ready to support President in Vietnam War, 1961-1975 Draft.**" Thirty-sixth and Locust Streets, Philadelphia, PA, February 11, 1980. Special Collections Research Center, Temple University Libraries, Philadelphia, PA. George D. McDowell *Philadelphia Evening Bulletin* Collection. ID: UAP168008. Accessed on 9/22/20 at https://digital.library.temple.edu/digital/collection/p15037coll3/id/7619/rec/1. Used with permission.

p. 6. Author Photo. "**Joe at Camp Evans with Platoon.**"

p. 9. Author Photo. "**Joe in front of S-4 bunker, Camp Evans, Vietnam.**"

p. 13. __. "**5 Presidents Who Served During the Vietnam War.**" Accessed 9/10/20 at https://www.thevietnamwar.info.

p. 19. Sauer, Jean-Claude. "**Vietnam, 1965.**" ARVN Soldiers and US Advisors. Joint operations between US special forces and government Vietnamese forces against the Vietcong around the Bu Dop post, about 1,500 m from the bird's-eye view of the Cambodian border and 135 km from Saigon. A group of American soldiers in the middle of a plain, with a helicopter landing in the background. July, 1965. Foter.com/manhhai. Accessed on 9/12/20 at https://foter.com/ffff/photo/45806284372/302d427d67/. CC BY 2.0.

p. 20. __. "**Airlifted Troops Mekong River Delta.**" 1962. South Vietnamese troops helicopter airlifted to attack Viet Cong. Foter.com/manhhai. Accessed on 9/12/20 at https://foter.com/ffff/photo/8266096716/b60cbae9b4/. CC BY 2.0.

p. 21. Glinn, Burt. "**Monks and others sitting in protest.**" August 19,

Vietnam Anti-War Movement—the Great American Con Job

1963. Foter.com/manhhai. Accessed on 9/12/20 at https://foter.com/ffff/photo/25713334236/fd9865e401/. CC BY 2.0.

p. 23. __. "**1966 Army Aviation.**" Helicopters Hover Over Vietnamese Troops. Foter.com/manhhai. Accessed on 9/14/20 at https://foter.com/ffff/photo/8265061709/f9e7dd31b3/. CC BY 2.0.

p. 23. __. "**Flight Of Huey Gunships.**" Vietnam, 1967. A flight of Hueys moves into the landing zone to disembark its troops. Each one hovers less than six seconds as the troops hit the ground running and disappear among the trees. Underwood Archives/UIG/Everett Collection. (4-War-VN-US-A-HA_5HR) UIGA010 XU934. Used with permission.

p. 24. Dung, James K. F. SFC. "**U.S. Army Bell UH-1D helicopters.**" 1966. U.S. Army Bell UH-1D helicopters airlift members of the 2nd Battalion, 14th Infantry Regiment from the Filhol Rubber Plantation area to a new staging area, during Operation "Wahiawa", a search and destroy mission conducted by the 25th Infantry Division, northeast of Cu Chi, South Vietnam, 1966. NARA. US Army. Accessed on Wikipedia on 10/02/20 at https://en.wikipedia.org/wiki/File:UH-1D_helicopters_in_Vietnam_1966.jpg. Public domain.

p. 27. __. "**University of Michigan students 'sit-in' at Administration Building.**" November 5, 1968. Foter.com/In Memoriam: Wystan. Accessed on 9/12/20 at https://foter.com/ffff/photo/8120128229/f63f9ccd82/. CC BY-SA.

p. 28. Jones, Laura; Phillips, Bennett Jones. "**Draft dodgers being counseled, 1967.**" Draft-age Americans being counseled by Mark Satin (far left) at the Anti-Draft Programme office on Spadina Avenue in Toronto, August, 1967. The front room was so crowded by Vietnam War resisters at the time that the counseling session here is taking place in one of the small side rooms. Accessed on accessed 9/22/20 at Wikimedia Commons contributors, Wikimedia Commons, the free media repository, https://commons.wikimedia.org/w/index.php?title=File:Draft_dodgers_being_counseled_1967.jpg&oldid=445341332. CC BY-SA 3.0.

p. 31. O'Halloran, Thomas J,; Trikosko, Marion S. "**Protesters. Government workers and hippies at the Capitol.**" May 5, 1971. Library of Congress. RN: LC-DIG-ppmsca-5043. CN: LC-U9-24390- 26A/27. Accessed on 9/27/20 at https://www.loc.gov/pictures/item/2017646307/. No known restrictions on publication.

p. 32. Baker, Lieutenant W. H. "**Troops leaving UH-1 helicopter.**" September, 1971. Naval Weapons Laboratory, Dahigren, Virgina. Accessed on Wikipedia on 9/26/20 at https://en.wikipedia.org/wiki/File:Troops_leaving_UH-1_copter.jpg. Public domain.

p. 37. __. "**Zelfverbrandingen in Vietnam.**" October 5, 1963. Spectators watch as flames engulf young Buddhist monk as he commits ritual suicide on Saigon's Market St. in this 10/5/1963 photo, protesting the government's religious policies. Self-immolation became a tactic of some demonstrators during the Vietnam War. Foter.com/manhhai. Accessed on Foter.com on 9/10/20 at https://foter.com/ffff/photo/25713334236/fd9865e401/. CC BY 2.0.

p. 41. Lourd, Tim. "**Students for a Democratic Society (SDS) logo.**" Accessed on Creative Commons 8/31/20. https://en.wikipedia.org/wiki/File:SDS_Logo.jpg. CC BY-SA 3.0.

p. 43. Leffler, Warren K. "**Oct. 15 Rally at Selective Service**" October 15, 1969. Library of Congress. RN: LC-DIG-ppmsca-56777. CN: LC-U9-21638-11. Accessed on 9/10/20 at https://www.loc.gov/pictures/item/2019636776/. No known restrictions on publication.

p. 47 __. "**Girls Say Yes to Boys Who Say No**" poster. Retro AdArchives/Alamy.com. Used with permission.

p. 47. __. "**Women Power.**" Accessed on DameMagazine.com on June 5, 2014. 8/31/20 at: https://www.damemagazine.com/wp-content/uploads/2017/09/NY-MARCH-08-26-1971.jpg.

Vietnam Anti-War Movement—the Great American Con Job

p. 49. Rosenberg, Ira. "**Muhammad Ali in 1967.**" *World Journal Tribune.* New York World-Telegram & Sun Newspaper Collection. Library of Congress. RN: LC-USZ62-115435. CN: NYWTS-BIOG. Accessed on 10/02/20 at https://www.loc.gov/pictures/item/96500238/. No known restrictions on publication.

p. 49. Levy, Builder. "**No Vietnamese Ever Called Me Nigger.**" April 27, 1967. Demonstration at the Harlem Peace March to End Racial Oppression. Taken from Muhammad Ali's statement regarding his refusal to participate in the Vietnam War. Amistad Resource, accessed 8/31/20 at https://www.amistadresource.org/civil_rights_era/archives/image_archive.html

p. 51. Leffler, Warren K. "**Martin Luther King Press conf.**" March 2, 1965. Library of Congress. RN: LC-DIG-ppmsca-49864. CN: LC-U9-13396-8. Accessed on 9/10/20 at https://www.loc.gov/pictures/item/2016646651/. No known restrictions on publication.

p. 51. ___. "**Dr. Benjamin Spock, Martin Luther King, Jr.**" Led nearly 5,000 marchers through the Chicago Loop to protest U.S. policy in Vietnam. March 25, 1967. Everette Collection. CSU Archives. Alamy.com. Used with permission.

p. 53. Wolfe, Frank. NARA. "**Vietnam War Protest in Washington, D.C.**" October 21, 1967. (Sign: "Get the Hell Out of Vietnam.") LBJ-WHPO: White House Photo Office Collection, 11/22/1963 - 01/20/1969 ARC Identifier: 192603. https://www.flickr.com/photos/39735679@N00/272804879. Public Domain.

p. 55. Ryan, Jim. "**We won't fight a rich man's war.**" 1976. Philadelphia Bicentenial Celebration. Accessed on 9/22/20 at https://tonimoore1.wordpress.com/2010/10/16/journalism-what-value-does-it-have-anyway/.

p. 55. ___. "**Resist the Draft, Don't Register.**" Marchers protest the draft. Accessed on 10/02/10 at https://sites.psu.edu/rclicopter/2018/10/05/with-the-first-overall-pick-in-the-united-states-military-draft/.

p. 57. Leffler, Warren K. "**Large crowd at a National Mobilization to End the War in Vietnam direct action demonstration.**" Washington, D.C. / WKL. October 21, 1967. Library of Congress. RN: LC-DIG-ds-07432. CN: LC-U9-18187- 4A. Accessed on 9/10/20 at https://www.loc.gov/pictures/item/2015647173/. No known restrictions on publication.

p. 59. Wolfe, Frank. "**Protesting the Vietnam War.**" October 21, 1967. National Archives (NARA). https://www.flickr.com/photos/39735679@N00/272805153. Public Domain.

p. 57. Leffler, Warren K. "**Anti-Vietnam War protest and demonstration in front of the White House in support of singer Eartha Kitt** / WKL or TO'H." January 19, 1968. Library of Congress. RN: LC-DIG-ppmsca-24360. CN: LC-U9-18528, frame 26. Accessed on 9/10/20 at https://www.loc.gov/pictures/item/2010646065/. No known restrictions on publication.

p. 61. Pasquarella, Dominic. "**Anti-war parade and rally marches toward Washington Square.**" April 27,1968. Sixth and Walnut Streets, Philadelphia, PA. Special Collections Research Center, Temple University Libraries, Philadelphia, PA. George D. McDowell *Philadelphia Evening Bulletin* Collection. ID P169276B. Accessed on 9/22/20 at https://digital.library.temple.edu/digital/collection/p15037coll3/id/22833/rec/56. Used with permission.

p. 61. Leffler, Warren K. "**Martin Luther King, Jr.,** head-and-shoulders portrait, facing right, at microphones, after? meeting with President Johnson to discuss civil rights, at the White House, 1963 / WKL." December 3, 1963. Library of Congress. RN: LC-DIG-ds-00836. CN: LC-U9- 10978-A-3. Accessed on 9/10/20 at https://www.loc.gov/pictures/item/2011648312/. No known restrictions on publication.

p. 65. ___ . "**Black Panthers on steps of legislative building, Olympia, WA.**" 1969. Washington State Archives, State Governors' Negative Collection, 1949-1975. (#4076.) On February 28, 1969, a group of Seattle Panthers led by Lt. Elmer Dixon gathered on the steps of the Capitol in Olympia to protest a bill that would make it a crime to exhibit firearms

Vietnam Anti-War Movement—the Great American Con Job

"in a manner manifesting an intent to intimidate others." In contrast to a California demonstration, they did not enter the building and they were not arrested. https://www.digitalarchives.wa.gov/Record/View/F4335BFEDE59686C55B7D39E38C1E07D. Public domain.

p. 65. Brown, Tim. "**Protesters play patriotic songs on kazoos at the anti-Vietnam War rally in Washington, DC.**" May 9, 1970. Protesters play patriotic songs on kazoos at the anti-Vietnam War rally in Washington, DC, May 9, 1970. An estimated 100,000 demonstrators converged to protest the fatal shootings at Kent State University and the American military incursion into Cambodia. Alamy.com. ID: HJARNP. Used with permission.

p. 67. p. Wasko, Joseph. "**Two men burning draft cards at Moratorium Rally at J.F.K. Plaza.**" 1969. Temple University Libraries, Special Collections Research Center. George D. McDowell *Philadelphia Evening Bulletin* Collection. ID SCRC 170. Accessed on 9/22/20 at https://digital.library.temple.edu/digital/collection/p15037coll3/id/7621/rec/121. Used with permission.

p. 67. Upton, Maurice M. "**Crowd of Vietnam War protesters at City Hall.**" September 9, 1969. Philadelphia, PA. Special Collections Research Center, Temple University Libraries, Philadelphia, PA. George D. McDowell *Philadelphia Evening Bulletin* Collection. ID: P169313B. Accessed on 9/22/20 at https://digital.library.temple.edu/digital/collection/p15037coll3/id/22866/rec/2. Used with permission.

p. 68. Leffler, Warren K. "**Draft Lottery**" August 5, 1971. Library of Congress. RN: LC-DIG-ppmsca-50470. CN: LC-U9-24745- 33/33A. Accessed on 9/10/20 at https://www.loc.gov/pictures/item/2017646351/. No known restrictions on publication.

p. 69. Tolliver, Lafayette. "**Vietnam War Moratorium Protest.**" October 15, 1969. Kent State University Libraries. Special Collections and Archives. Accessed September 5, 2020 at https://omeka.library.kent.edu/special-collections/items/show/7683. Used with permission.

Joe Abodeely

p. 69. Leffler, Warren K. "**October 15 Peace Moratorium,**" October 15, 1969. Library of Congress. RN: LC-DIG-ppmsca-56775. CN: LC-U9-21608-33. Accessed on 9/10/20 at https://www.loc.gov/pictures/item/2019636774/. No known restrictions on publication.

p. 71. St. John, Marmaduke. "**Viet Cong flags frame anti-Vietnam War protesters in Boston.**" April, 1970. Note Black Panthers flag at upper right. Alamy.com. ID: B8XJ99. Used with permission.

p. 71. __. "**Members of the Chicago Conspiracy, Abbie Hoffman and Jim Rubin, (center), New Haven, Conneticut.**" 1970. CSU Archives / Everett Collection. Alamy.com ID: BTJGA6. Used with permission.

p. 73. Kent State University News Service. "**National Guard personnel walking toward crowd near Taylor Hall, tear gas has been fired,**" Kent State University Libraries. Special Collections and Archives, accessed August 29, 2020, https://omeka.library.kent.edu/special-collections/items/show/1427. ID: 705/4-1-35. Used with permission

p. 73. Kent State University News Service. "**National Guard personnel wearing gas masks, holding rifles,**" Kent State University Libraries. Special Collections and Archives, accessed September 2, 2020, https://omeka.library.kent.edu/special-collections/items/show/1427. ID: 705/4-1-22. Used with permission.

p. 75. Upton, Maurice M. "**Rally-ist with home made signs.**" April 15, 1970. Philacdelphia, PA. Special Collections Research Center, Temple University Libraries, Philadelphia, PA. George D. McDowell *Philadelphia Evening Bulletin* Collection. ID: P169329B. Accessed on 9/22/20 at https://digital.library.temple.edu/digital/collection/p15037coll3/id/22881/rec/104. Used with permission.

p. 75. Adler, Harold. "**An anti-Vietnam War peace march up Geary Boulevard with Vietnam vets and United Prisoners Union advocates leading the way.**" San Francisco, California. 1970. Underwood Archives. Alamy.com. Image ID: P1W21H. Used with permission.

Vietnam Anti-War Movement—the Great American Con Job

p. 77. Leffler, Warren K. "**John Kerry spokesman for VVAW.**" Washington D.C, April 21, 1970. https://www.loc.gov/item/2003673992/. RN: LC-DIG-ppmsca-50415. CN: LC-U9-24273-12A.) Accessed on 9/10/20 at https://www.loc.gov/pictures/item/2017646291/. No known restrictions on publication.

p. 79. __. "**Vietnam Veterans Against the War.**" Chicago, October 25, 1971. Vietnam Veterans Against the War (VVAW), *The Veteran*, Fall, 2014. Photo titled "halgash_nixon_chi_3-15-74." Accessed on 9/20/20 at http://www.vvaw.org/veteran/article/?id=2867.

p. 79. __. Newspix. "**Melbourne, Australia. Over 200,000 people gathered across the country to protest the Vietnam War.**" Adelaide, South Australia, May, 1970. A moratorium march protesting against Australia's involvement in the Vietnam War. News Ltd / Newspix. Photo ID: NP12883. Used with permission.

p. 81. Moldenhauer, Jearld. "**Gay women protesting the war.**" Accessed on 9/18/20 at https://www.jearldmoldenhauer.com/demonstration-against-vietnam-war-nov-6-1971/nggallery/slideshow. Used with permission.

p. 81. Lane, Bettye. "**A Women's Liberation demonstration against the Vietnam War.**" 1972. Science History Images. Alamy.com. ID: HRF7XB. Used with permission.

p. 83. "**Jane Fonda in Hanoi**." July 25, 1972. Foter.com/manhhai. Accessed 9/10/20 at https://foter.com/ffff/photo/ 25402471323/afb0460c1e/. CC BY 2.0.

p. 88. Hamilton. "**Parade forms outside City Hall.**" Philadelphia, PA, October, 24, 1965. Parade forms--American Legion and Veterans of Foreign War members meet at City Hall for a 'Dedication Day' parade to Independence Hall in support of US policy on Vietnam. Special Collections Research Center, Temple University Libraries, Philadelphia, PA. George D. McDowell *Philadelphia Evening Bulletin* Collection. ID:

Joe Abodeely

P169253B. Accessed on 9/22/20 at https://digital.library.temple.edu/digital/collection/p15037coll3/id/22811/rec/29. Used with permission.

p. 90. Leffler, Warren K.; O'Halloran, Thomas J. "**Women's Equal Rights Parade**" August 26, 1977. Library of Congress. RN: LC-DIG-ppmsca-55373. CN: LC-U9-35056-16. Accessed on 9/10/20 at https://www.loc.gov/pictures/item/2018645703/. No known restrictions on publication.

p. 90. Allen, Elmer, People's World. "**Seattle Chicanos lead Peace March**," October 31, 1970. Part of the Harry Bridges Center for Labor Studies collection. Accessed on 9/20/20 at https://depts.washington.edu/civilr/mecha_photos.htm.

p 91. Leffler, Warren K.; O'Halloran, Thomas J. "**Black Panther Convention, Lincoln Memorial** / [TOH/WKL]." June 19, 1970. Library of Congress. RN: LC-DIG-ppmsca-04303. CN: LC-U9-22860-27. Accessed on 9/10/20 at https://www.loc.gov/pictures/item/2003688170/. No known restrictions on publication.

p. 91. Leffler, Warren K. "**Black demonstration in Washington, D.C. Justice Dept. Bobby Kennedy speaking to crowd** / [WKL]." June 14, 1963. Library of Congress. RN: LC-DIG-ppmsca-04295. CN: LC-U9- 9956-30. Accessed on 9/18/20 at https://www.loc.gov/pictures/item/2003688162/. No known restrictions on publication.

p. 97. Leffler, Warren K, photographer. "**Civil rights march on Washington, D.C.** / [WKL]." Washington D.C, August 28, 1963. A crowd of Blacks and Whites surrounding the Reflecting Pool and continuing to the Washington Monument. Library of Congress. RN: LC-DIG-ppmsca-03130. Call Number. LC-U9- 10363-5. Accessed on 9/22/20 at https://www.loc.gov/pictures/resource/ppmsca.03130/. No known restrictions on publication.

p. 97. Leffler, Warren K. "**Civil rights march on Washington, D.C.** [WKL]." August 28, 1963. A procession of African Americans carrying signs for equal rights, integrated schools, decent housing, and an end to bias. Library of Congress. RN: LC-DIG-ppmsca-03128. CN: LC-U9-10364-37.

Vietnam Anti-War Movement—the Great American Con Job

Accessed on 9/18/20 at https://www.loc.gov/item/2003654393/. No known restrictions on publication.

p. 102. __. US Army. "**US Army Major Bruce Crandall flies his UH-1D helicopter after discharging a load of infantrymen on a search and destroy mission during the Battle of Ia Drang, Vietnam.**" November 14, 1965. Accessed on Wikimedia Commons on 9/26/20 at https://commons.wikimedia.org/wiki/File:Bruce_Crandall%27s_UH-1D.jpg. Public Domain.

p. 102. Lange, Katie. US Army Photo. "**Soldiers with the Army's 1st Cavalry Division disembark a UH-1 Iroquois helicopter in the Ia Drang Valley.**" Battle of Ia Drang. Accessed at dvidshub.net on 9/18/20 at https://www.dvidshub.net/image/5292652/vietnam-war-ia-drang-valley-battle-ia-drang-1st-cavalry-division-uh-1.

p. 104. __. US Army. "**A U.S. Army rifle squad from the Blue Team of the 1st Squadron, 9th Cavalry exiting from a Bell UH-1D Huey helicopter in Vietnam.**" The 1st Squadron, 9th Cavalry Regiment was the air cavalry reconnaissance squadron of the 1st Cavalry Division throughout the division's service in Vietnam from 1965 to 1972. The "Blue Team" were UH-1 troop transport helicopters, the "Red Team" were UH-1 gunships, the "White Team" Scouts were OH 13 Bell Helicopters, (Low and Slow). Accessed on Wikipedia on 9/26/20 at https://commons.wikimedia.org/wiki/File:Infantry_1-9_US_Cavalry_exiting_UH-1D.jpg. Public domain.

p. 105. __. "**Army Airborne In Vietnam.**" Ben Hoa, Vietnam: 1967. U.S. Army Airborne soldiers move through Viet Cong sniper fire toward the jungle after being dropped by Hueys in a rice field. Underwood Archives/UIG/Everett Collection. (4-War-VN-US-A-HA_4HR) UIGA010 XU933. Used with permission.

p. 112. __. "**Mass dead at Hue after occupation.**" 1968. In the aftermath of the recapture of Hue in 1968, the discovery of several mass graves of South Vietnamese citizens of Hue sparked a controversy that has not diminished with time. The official allied explanation was that during occupation of the city hostiles to the communists were executed. Later the press revealed 'revenge squads" against those who had assisted the communists. The truth may never be known. Pictures from History / CPA Media Pte Ltd. Alamy.com Image ID: 2B01FJ5. Used with permission.

p. 121. __. "**Brigadier General Lê Minh Đảo.**" Marked as "Courtesy of KBC-Hain Goai." Accessed on Wikipedia on 9/14/20 at https://en.wikipedia.org/wiki/L%C3%AA_Minh_%C4%90%E1%BA%A3o#/media/File:Xuanloc_18th.jpg. Public domain.

p. 129. __. "**Hue Citadel.**" Vietnam tourist photo accessed 9/5/20 at http://hanoisplendidhotel.com/DAILY-TRIPS/Hue-City-1-Day-Top-choice.

p. 130. Sauer, Jean-Claude. "**A group of armed Vietnamese military tankers in their tanks.**" Vietnam, August 30, 1968. Foter.com/manhhai. Accessed on 9/14/20 at https://foter.com/ffff/photo/45806284352/44e07d6733/. CC BY 2.0.

p. 131. Whiting, Charles. "**The 8 inch, M110 Self-Propelled Howitzer.**" Accessed on Wikipedia on 9/28/20 at https://search.creativecommons.org/photos/95a705e6-bbfa-4b53-acba-73906796c9a1. CC BY 2.0.

p. 131. __. "**Tank, M113 w/soldiers on the road.**" 1960. Vietnam War. Soldiers on dirt road in M113 APC. Foter.com/manhhai. Accessed on Foter.com on 9/12/20 at https://foter.com/ffff/photo/22413357441/325e734f36/. CC BY 2.0.

p. 132. Messenger, Lance Corporal D. M. "**Close Surveillance: A marine observation plane makes a low level pass over Hue during recent action in the Imperial City.**" February 23, 1968. USMC. Jonathan Abel Collection (COLL/3611). Accessed on Wikipedia 9/28/20 at https://en.wikipedia.org/wiki/File:Marine_Observation_Plane,_23_February_1968_(15808124453)_(cropped).jpg. CC BY 2.0.

p. 133. __. "**1st Cavalry Division helicopter resupply mission northwest of Hue.**" February, 17, 1968. US. Army. Accessed on Wikipedia on 9/28/20 at https://en.wikipedia.org/wiki/File:1st_Cavalry_Division_helicopter_resupply_mission_northwest_of_Hue.jpg. Public domain.

p. 148. __. "**Khe Sanh, Vietnam, air strip.**" The airstrip was built in September 1962. Fighting began there in late April of 1967 known as the 'Hill Fights', which later expanded into the 1968 Battle of Khe Sanh. Pictures from History. CPA Media Pte Ltd. Alamy.com. ID: 2B01P3W. Used with permission.

p 151. Khe Sanh, Vietnam map.

p. 152. __. Pictures from History. "**Marines battle at Khe Sanh.**" CPA Media Pte Ltd. Alamy.com. ID: 2B01P3N. Used with permission.

p. 154. __. "**LZ Cà Lu (Stud).**" 1st Cav forces at Landing Zone Cà Lu (Stud), the staging area for Operation Pegasus. April 4, 1968. manhhai. Accessed on Creative Commons 9/14/20 at https://search.creativecommons.org/photos/ae6f9941-7589-4d14-9bb2-4165a1b22570. CC BY 2.0.

p. 155. Dang, Phuoc Van. "**Operation Pegasus.**" 1968. Associated Press photo. ID: 6804050711. Used with permission.

p. 156. Sauer, Jean-Claude. "**Man carrying a recoilless rifle.**" July 18, 1965. The U.S. Marines during an operation: the attack on the village of LIMY. An American soldier crossing a field in the Vietnamese countryside, a bazooka under his arm. Foter.com/manhhai. Accessed on 9/14/20 at https://foter.com/ffff/photo/45823476662/4e8d045c42/. CC BY 2.0.

p. 161. __. "**Vietnam Chinook.**" Wikimedia Commons contributors, "File:Ch47-chinook-vietnam.jpg," Accessed on 9/16/20 at https://commons.wikimedia.org/w/index.php?title=File:Ch47-chinook-vietnam.jpg&oldid=339047471. Public Domain.

p. 165. Lutz, Robert. "**1st Cav Operation Pegasus.**" Robert Lutz Collection. Used with permission.

Joe Abodeely

p. 167. Lutz, Robert. "**NVA mortar rounds and arms.**" (2 photos) Robert Lutz Collection. Used with permission.

p. 168. Author Photo. "**NVA Bugle captured near Khe Sanh.**"

p. 171. Nalty, Bernard C. "**The fight for Khe Sanh,**" Special Studies, Washington, DC: Office of Air Force History, United States Air Force, p. 100. Soldiers of the 1st Cavalry Division moving towards Khe Sanh Combat Base during Operation Pegasus. Accessed on Creative Commons on 9/5/20 at https://commons.wikimedia.org/wiki/File:Khe_Sanh_Operation_Pegasus_First_Cavalry.jpg. Public domain.

p. 171. Breedlove, SSG Howard C. "**Operation Pegasus U.S. marines stand by the road leading through Khe Sanh as members of Company "B", 5th Battalion, 7th Cavalry, 3rd Brigade, pass on their way to Hill 680.**" NARA. Accessed on Wikipedia on 9/26/20 at https://en.wikipedia.org/wiki/File:NARA_photo_111-CCV-557-CC47875.jpg. Public domain.

p. 173. Lutz, Robert. "**Nardi and Lutz with Khe Sanh Sign.**" Robert Lutz Collection. Used with permission.

p. 175. Author Photo. "**2nd Platoon D/2/7, 1st Cavalry Division (Airmobile).**"

p. 182. O'Halloran, Thomas J. "**Walter Cronkite on television during 1st presidential debate between Ford and Carter, Philadelphia, Pennsylvania.**" September 23, 1976. Library of Congress. RN: LC-DIG-ppmsca-08500. CN: LC-U9- 33387-16A. Accessed on 9/17/20 at https://www.loc.gov/pictures/item/2005684040/. No known restrictions on publication.

www.ingramcontent.com/pod-product-compliance
Lightning Source LLC
Chambersburg PA
CBHW070547010526
44118CB00012B/1256